MARY GRIFFITH

THE
Unschooling
Handbook

How to Use the

Whole World as Your

Child's Classroom

THREE RIVERS PRESS
NEW YORK

Copyright © 1998 by Mary Griffith

Published in the United States by Three Rivers Press, an imprint of the Crown Publishing Group, a division of Random House, Inc., New York.

THREE RIVERS PRESS and the Tugboat design are registered trademarks of Random House, Inc.

Originally published by Prima Publishing, Roseville, California, in 1998.

Library of Congress Cataloging-in-Publication Data

Griffith, Mary.
    The unschooling handbook: how to use the whole world as your child's classroom / Mary Griffith.
        p.   cm.
        Includes bibliographical references and index.
    1. Home schooling—United States.   2. Self-culture—United States.   3. Learning.
    4. Educational planning—United States.   I. Title.
    LC40.G755   1998
    371.04'2—dc21   98-121777
                                                                                              CIP

ISBN 0-7615-1276-4

Printed in the United States of America

www.crownpublishing.com

10 9 8

First Edition

CONTENTS

ACKNOWLEDGMENTS

I am always astounded by and grateful for the willingness of homeschooling families to share their experiences with other families. The unschoolers who helped with this book were as enthusiastic and articulate as any group I've worked with: Barbara Alward, Amy Bell, Terri Blessman, Cathy Koos Breazeal, Stefani Burk, Carol Burris, Lynda Burris, Jo Craddock, Laura Derrick, Sandra Dodd, Cindy Duckert, Carol Edson, Carolyn Ellis, Samantha Fenner, Joyce Fetteroll, Emilie Fogle, Melissa Hatheway, Lillian Jones, Susan Johnson Knotts, Marianne Marshall, Patrick McLaughlin, Liane Peterson, Ruth Rohde, Cathy Russell, Andrea Shakal, Terry Stafford, Grace Sylvan, Joanne Turner, Kathy Wentz, Linda Wyatt, and Laura Young. Most wrote at length in response to my questionnaire (a daunting one that I never quite got around to answering myself), and several even thanked me for the opportunity to think seriously about their approach to learning. Reading all they wrote has been one of the real pleasures of working on this book.

I'm also indebted to the many homeschooling friends and colleagues whose contributions took less tangible form—most often as conversations that provoked new ideas: Jill Boone, Diana Broughton, Karl Bunday, Micki and David Colfax, Barbara David, Pam Davis, Pat Farenga, Bill and Nancy Greer, Helen and Mark Hegener, Diane Kallas, Lanis LeBaron, Donna Nichols-White, Kim and Julie Stuffelbeam, and Anne Wasserman. In the same vein, my thanks go to: the "skate days" gang at the Homeschooling Co-op of Sacramento; the rowdy, often contentious, and always absorbing individuals who comprise the Home Ed, Unschooling, and Radical Unschooling lists on the Internet; and the dozens of parents who ask all those penetrating and incisive questions at conference workshops.

The folks at Prima—Jamie Miller, Leslie Eschen, and Robin Lockwood—once again made the whole process of turning a raw manuscript into a finished book seem easy.

Finally, my daughters have been indispensable throughout this project, and not simply as general inspiration. Kate faithfully kept me to my schedule ("Have you written today's thousand words yet, Mom?"), and Christie made sure I paid attention to the rest of the world ("Mom, don't you think it's time you did something besides writing today?"). Both continue to make life interesting.

INTRODUCTION

The popular image of homeschooling usually involves several neatly dressed, hypernaturally polite and disciplined children sitting around a kitchen table, diligently working at spelling lists, multiplication tables, and sentence diagrams. Mom, who bears a remarkable resemblance to June Cleaver, hovers in the background, ready to jump in with advice, assistance, and supervision the instant she's needed.

Perhaps it's that word—"homeschooling"—or perhaps it's just that most of us grew up going to conventional schools, but we Americans have a hard time imagining any form of education that doesn't look a lot like school, albeit on a smaller scale. But until the turn of the nineteenth century, most American children got the better part of their education in ways much closer to those used by homeschoolers today than those found in modern public schools.

Until the advent of the "common school" movement in the 1850s, which culminated in compulsory attendance statutes nationwide by the turn of the century, school was optional for most families. Formal attendance at school was often confined to the winter months when the pace of life slowed and children were comparatively free of agricultural chores. Furthermore, unless a child was male and planned to go to college or a seminary—or came from a well-to-do family—school only lasted for three to five years. That provided just enough time to get a good grasp of reading, writing, and arithmetic, with a smattering of history and literature. The rest of the knowledge children needed to become competent adults was acquired by working alongside older family members or other adults, learning everyday tasks by doing them, knowing that their work was an essential contribution to their family's livelihood.

Along with the widespread establishment of public schools and compulsory attendance laws came an equally widespread belief in schools as essential for children to learn to function as citizens in twentieth-century society. So much were schools assumed to be necessary for children's education that, while there was much debate over the form schools should take and the content they should teach, there was almost no discussion of whether they were in truth the indispensable institutions they appeared to be. Those few children who somehow acquired their education mainly by other means, of whom Margaret Mead and Thomas Edison were notable examples, were viewed as eccentric exceptions.

But those exceptions nevertheless existed. Some children simply lived in remote settings, too far from established schools to make attendance practical. Other children—Edison, for example—simply found school intolerable or came from families with unconventional ideas about learning. Mead's quip was, "My grandmother wanted me to have an education, so she kept me out of school."

These unconventional learners took a variety of paths for their education. Some had formal tutors to present material their families thought necessary for their education. Some read widely and voraciously. Others accompanied their parents in their work or on their travels; their "lessons" were simply side effects of the way they spent their time.

Whatever circumstances led to their unconventional approaches to education, though, these independent learners were isolated cases. Homeschooling did not become a movement until the 1970s, when educator John Holt, disillusioned with the process of school reform, began publicly advocating homeschooling. Holt became convinced that the kind of child-centered educational reforms he believed were necessary would not—indeed, could not—happen within a compul-

> So much were schools assumed to be necessary for children's education that, while there was much debate over the form schools should take and the content they should teach, there was almost no discussion of whether they were in truth the indispensable institutions they appeared to be.

sory school setting. In 1977, Holt began publishing a four-page newsletter called *Growing Without Schooling* for families who wanted ideas and support to help their children learn outside of school. Holt's ideas struck a chord with many parents who thought along similar lines. Within six months, *GWS* (as it almost immediately became known) had nearly five hundred subscribers; Holt's appearance on *The Phil Donahue Show* a couple of years later prompted almost ten thousand letters asking for more information.

Holt originally used the word "unschooling" to describe the act of removing one's children from school, but it soon became a synonym for "homeschooling." Over the past two decades, the meaning of the term has evolved and narrowed, so that "unschooling" now refers to the specific style of homeschooling that Holt advocated, based on child-centered learning.

Since the 1970s the homeschooling movement has grown enormously. Some sources estimate that in the United States as many as 1.5 to 2 million students are homeschooled. Since the laws regulating homeschooling—and therefore the legal definitions of the term "homeschooler"—vary widely from state to state, accurate estimates are hard to come by. Breaking the movement into categories based on the style of homeschooling is even more difficult, and estimates of the numbers of homeschoolers who consider themselves unschoolers differ according to whom you ask. What we can say is that unschoolers constitute somewhere between ten and fifty percent of the movement.

> Since the 1970s the homeschooling movement has grown enormously. Some sources estimate that in the United States as many as 1.5 to 2 million students are homeschooled.

Traditionally, homeschoolers who take a fairly conventional approach to education, using more or less formal curriculum packages according to a relatively fixed schedule, have tended to frown on unschooling. They view it as a form of benign neglect at best, and sometimes publicly criticize unschoolers as giving homeschooling a bad name.

But such staunch traditionalists often find themselves moving toward the less formal approach as they discover its advantages for their families.

I tried to do "school at home" at first, but didn't like the amount of coercion I had to use to get anything done. We probably tried to keep some structure for a year or more, but slid into unschooling the end of last year. —*Stefani*, New Hampshire

We always knew we would homeschool, but we really geared up for it when Susie, our oldest, turned five. We spent about two weeks with me making up a bare-bones lesson plan, and then either abandoning it completely or making all of us miserable trying to follow it. So then I gave up and decided she was already brilliant enough to figure things out for herself. It was about six months after this that I discovered there was a term "unschooling." —*Amy*, Idaho

I was very anxious and uncertain the first year, so I set up my own curriculum and followed it rigidly. I burned out very badly by the following summer, but managed to do the same thing for the fourth grade. After that, the entire thing just began metamorphosing into another entity. I'd successfully taught the girls multiplication (without memorization) and division, and felt I'd answered my critics sufficiently. Also, the girls began to really resist certain things, so I backed off happily. I got a couple of textbooks, for form's sake, but relieved myself (and the kids, too) of most duties for that next year. It's been a long process of unraveling the school protocol; with each year we feel more free of its shadow, until now it seems like an alien thing, even the concept of it. —*Liane*, California

So What Exactly Is Unschooling?

Answering that question is what this book is all about. Unschoolers are no different from other homeschoolers in at least one sense: we love to talk about what we do and why; the few dozen of us you will read about in this book are no exception. We've found a style of child-rearing, an approach to education, a way of life that allows our children so many advantages over conventional schooling that it often sounds too simple and easy to be credible—too good to be true.

We often find ourselves confronted by skeptics who insist that unschooling has to be more complicated than we say it is, that there must be some key element we are leaving out.

> We've found a style of child-rearing, an approach to education, a way of life that allows our children so many advantages over conventional schooling that it often sounds too simple and easy to be credible—too good to be true.

But the essence of unschooling is that there is no magic formula, no simple solution-in-a-box for every child's educational problem. Unschooling is simply a way to tailor learning to the specific needs of each child and each family. No two unschooling families follow the same path—and no two children within the same unschooling family are likely to go exactly in the same direction.

So we won't provide you with an easy-to-follow master plan guaranteed to turn your children into geniuses or get them into the Ivy League colleges of their choice. What we will do is tell you how we've approached the learning process with our kids, and what works and doesn't work for us. We don't have any mysterious curricula or magical techniques that will provide all the answers your family is seeking. What we do have is experience and a lot of ideas about how people learn and how to help them do so.

The first four chapters give an overview of unschooling. Chapter 1 tells how we define unschooling and how we view learning and our children, and looks at the research support for an unschooling approach to education. Chapter 2 covers the materials we learn from: everything from traditional curricular materials, toys, and games, to friends and acquaintances, to completely unconventional learning resources. In Chapter 3, we'll look at learning and technology—at the uses of television, videos, and computers in learning with our kids, and at some of the debate over their value. In Chapter 4, we'll talk about evaluating and documenting the whole process: how can we tell our kids are learning?

The next five chapters give examples of unschooling approaches to learning in basic subject areas: reading and writing; mathematics, logic, and problem-solving; the sciences; history and the social sciences; and the fine and performing arts. You'll find that these subject divisions are somewhat arbitrary; many of the topics or activities our children pursue fall easily into two or three areas simultaneously. However, these chapters should begin to give you an idea of the process of unschooling.

> But the essence of unschooling is that there is no magic formula, no simple solution-in-a-box for every child's educational problem. Unschooling is simply a way to tailor learning to the specific needs of each child and each family.

The final four chapters look at some of the larger issues involved with unschooling. Chapter 10 addresses typical changes in the unschooling process as our children grow older and more independent, and considers the future beyond family-based learning. Chapter 11 introduces the practical considerations of legalities, siblings, and managing time and money. Chapter 12 looks at some of the ways to find help and support for an unschooling approach to learning. Finally, Chapter 13 considers some of the societal implications of the unschooling approach: How does it affect family life? What are its long-term consequences? Can conventional educators learn anything from unschoolers?

By the time you reach the end of this book, we hope we will have provoked lots of questions in your mind, and piqued your interest in starting to find the answers that will work for your family. Even if you ultimately choose a more conventional educational approach, we hope that our experience will get you thinking in new ways about learning, about your children, and about helping your children explore their world.

CHAPTER ONE

What Is Unschooling and How Can It Possibly Work?

I MAGINE TWO STUDENTS, each about fifteen years old, seated at a table working on geometry problems. They are both using paper and pencil, perhaps a ruler and compass, and the same textbook. To all outward appearances, each is doing exactly the same thing as the other. But one is an unschooler and the other is conventionally schooled.

What's the difference? To understand that difference, we need to look at the rest of these kids' lives, how they spend the bulk of their time, why they are working on geometry, and what they will do next and why.

Our school student—let's call her Cynthia—is pretty easy to understand since most of us went through roughly the same process when we were teens. Cynthia is enrolled in a local public high school, and geometry is one of the courses she signed up for last year. Most of the colleges she's considering attending recommend at least two, and preferably three or even four, years of mathematics at the high school level. Those problems she's working on were assigned by her teacher this morning, and, though she enjoys geometry and could easily spend a couple more hours playing around with angles and lines, she doesn't really have the time; she has to read a chapter in her world history textbook for tomorrow, and then she'll work on an English paper that's due by the end of the week. Next year, Cynthia will take another math course at her school—probably an algebra 2/trigonometry combination.

Kathleen, our unschooler, has never been to school. Early last spring when she helped her parents build some raised beds for their vegetable garden, she was intrigued when they measured the box diagonals to check that the corners were square. She asked lots of questions about angles and shapes while they worked together. Over the next few weeks, she began looking seriously into learning more about geometry. After a few more rambling conversations and a few trips to the library and local bookstores with her mother, she finally decided to use a textbook to dig into the topic formally. Over the past four or five weeks, she has worked on geometry fairly often, sometimes for several hours every day, sometimes for only a few minutes a couple of times a week between her dance lessons and the latest science fiction novel she's reading. She rarely completes a full problem set, opting to go on to the next concept as soon as she grasps an idea. Her brothers are getting heartily sick of her frequent geometry mini-lectures every time they get out their Lego blocks, but they grudgingly admit she's been building some amazingly complex designs lately (even though they really think she's too old to play with building toys). Kathleen has seen hints of the existence of non-Euclidean geometries in her textbook, and she's begun to look for a good introduction to topology. Her dad has offered to check around among some of his more mathematically inclined friends to see if anyone might be interested in working with her.

Unschooling is basically a matter of attitude and approach. Simply put, unschooling puts the learner in charge. As one California mother puts it:

Unschooling, to me, means learning what one wants, when one wants, in the way one wants, where one wants, for one's own reasons. The learning is learner-directed; advisors or facilitators are sought out as desired *by the learner*. There are no curricula, lesson plans, schedules, or agendas. Most of the learning is quiet, even invisible, as there is not a focus on creating a lot of "products." —*Carol*, California

Sounds impossible, doesn't it? The idea that children—even quite young children—should be in charge of their own education, choose what they learn and how they learn it, and even choose whether they should learn anything at all sounds ludicrous. Surely there must be more to the idea than that.

Listen to a few more parents describe their own concepts of unschooling:

Unschooling, for us, is mindful living, free play, and exploration. It is letting go of the schoolish "shoulds" and "oughts" and measuring sticks. We aim to live more fully rather than manufacture educational experiences to fill the gaps in our lives. Living this way requires a considerable amount of trust and patience—trust that children will learn what they need to know without years of conventional instruction, and patience enough to let them get to it in their own good time. It is not a life to be hurried, nor is it neat and tidy.

> Unschooling, to me, means learning what one wants, when one wants, in the way one wants, where one wants, for one's own reasons. The learning is learner-directed; advisors or facilitators are sought out as desired *by the learner.*

What we are doing is so vastly different from the way our society is schooled to believe humans learn that most people are quite skeptical, even uncomprehending of it. How do you know if they're learning? Do you use textbooks? How can you tell if they're at grade level? What about phonics? How will they get into college? How will they learn to do things they don't like to do? What about advanced math and science? The litany of questions makes me chuckle and then sigh. Understanding what it's all

about is a journey, not a one-paragraph definition. Even beginning to understand requires a willingness on the part of the questioner to deschool
a little. —*Laura D.,* Texas

We don't approach learning as something people do as a separate activity. We live our lives and learn as we go. We have no teaching, no classes,
no lesson plans, no grades, no curriculum, no textbooks, no tests. Basically, I
don't pay particular attention to what the kids are learning; it is enough to
see that they are growing as people, and gaining knowledge and experience as they go. I don't keep track of what they do, other than as you'd
know about what any of your friends learn about subjects they are interested in. We talk a lot. There is no special time set aside to do a learning activity, nor are any activities done because they're educational. I have no list,
physical or mental, of what I think they should know at any certain age.

We do a lot of learning, though. Our interests tend to be in things that
are frequently considered educational. The kids spend a lot of time using
the computer. Simon loves to read and spends a lot of his time reading.
Simon and Timmy both do a lot of writing. —*Linda,* New York

My whole philosophy of unschooling is based on the premise that
learning is a natural, enjoyable, impossible-to-avoid drive that we are
all born with. I believe that children want to learn about life and will learn
if they're not interfered with. By interference, I mean extrinsic rewards,
threats, being told what to learn and when to learn it.

You have to trust children in order to unschool.

The demands on families as far as time is concerned are "no time at
all" and "all the time in the world." We are unschooling twenty-four hours of
the day, but it doesn't take any extra time from what we'd be doing anyway. It's like asking how much time it takes to live. —*Susan,* Iowa

As a classroom teacher I was always amazed at how well the students
always did in the subject areas that sparked their interest. One good, well-
done demonstration could ensure better understanding from your students,

not because they understood the concepts but because they had become interested enough in it to want to learn about it. It became obvious to me that if a child wants to learn something, a child will learn it, and learn it very well. Unschooling, for us, taps into that natural curiosity and desire to learn.

I think the biggest misconception I've had to face about unschooling is that the parents have a totally hands-off attitude regarding their children. I have even been told that I must be ignoring my children, and that unschoolers have simply come up with a name in order to legitimize our abuse! I think it is the opposite, actually.

As an unschooler I find I spend quite a bit of time and energy helping my children. I am their facilitator. I am their guide through the library and resource books. I am their chauffeur and travel agent to exotic places. I am also the cleaner-upper of spilled paint, the answerer (for the hundredth time) of a math question, and the guide to the mysteries of their world.
—*Kathy*, Illinois

Q: Do you like unschooling?

RORY (8): Unschooling's just great. If I mess up on work, I'm able to take the time to get it right again. I think I'm learning more and it's better than school. I can't think of anything I'd like to do that I can't, and there are a lot of things I can do now that I couldn't do in school.

HALLIE (6): I feel better than I would in school, much better. 'Cause in school you can't see your parents as much as I can now. I very much enjoy learning this way. If I don't like a book, I can change to a different book.

Traits of the Unschooling Household

Because of the individualized nature of unschooling, no two unschooling households look exactly alike. There is no common schedule, no common curriculum, no common set of materials among unschooling families. In fact, because their interests may diverge radically, even the experiences of children in the same family can differ significantly.

Some families come upon unschooling while their children are still infants and deliberately set out to create circumstances under which unschooling can thrive. Others develop similar ideas and habits haphazardly in the process of searching for a form of education that works for their kids. However they come upon the approach, though, unschooling households have certain characteristics in common.

No two unschooling households look exactly alike. There is no common schedule, no common curriculum, no common set of materials among unschooling families. In fact, because their interests may diverge radically, even the experiences of children in the same family can differ significantly.

An Environment Conducive to Exploration and Experimentation

The first requirement is that children spend the bulk of their time in places where learning and exploration are possible and welcome. For some families, this may mean that their house is filled with books and toys and games and art supplies—with materials most of us think of as educational. For others, the emphasis may be on the equipment of everyday life: kitchen utensils and gardening tools, calculators and computers. The exact details of the surroundings matter little—after all, every family lives in different circumstances—but children need to feel comfortable exploring those surroundings and using what they find around them.

A farm family, for instance, might possess little in the way of manufactured "educational" supplies, but the farm itself—the animals, the tools, the crops, and the land—provide an abundance of opportunities to explore and experiment. The family may not even think of its setting as "educational," nor might the children think of the projects and chores they spend their time on as "learning." Likewise, an urban family might choose to emphasize the community as a source of learning opportunities, instead of filling their home with materials of more transitory interest. Whatever the nature of the environment, though, it is imperative that unschooling children have access to what interests them.

We sold the desks, and in their place put a large table (the big ugly warehouse kind) where we can spread out our projects. We took the supplies out of their boxes and put them on a set of low bookshelves (a little Montessori technique creeping in). I found things were actually being used! —*Jo, Louisiana*

> Whatever the nature of the environment, though, it is imperative that un-schooling children have access to what interests them.

I've always made sure that there was a rich body of knowledge available to our son. We have a house full of books and good software, we travel, we read together—often aloud. We've spent many, many hours together in good books, and we've gone to fascinating places together: the Grand Canyon, the Plymouth Colony, Williamsburg, California missions, sites from *Little House on the Prairie* books, the Smithsonian, castles in Great Britain—we drink it all in. —*Lillian, California*

It's not necessary to have a lot of stuff to unschool. We do have a huge library and all kinds of what I consider educational games and resources (jigsaw puzzles, abacuses, tangrams, crayons, clay, paints, paper, forest, creeks, yards, goats, dogs, turkeys, wildlife, flowers, gardens, tools, kitchen gear, etc.). I couldn't possibly list all the things my kids have learned from through the years. But this is all stuff that we would have anyway. It is not educational paraphernalia that we purchase specifically to homeschool. Dan and I like doing and learning and living, so we have lots of stuff around

to help us do that. The kids are welcome to use whatever of it they wish.
—*Susan, Iowa*

We'll look at finding and using learning resources in more detail in the next chapter.

Adults as Models and Facilitators

At least as important as material to learn about and from are people to learn from. Formal qualifications such as teaching credentials, undergraduate or advanced degrees, or early childhood education courses are unimportant. What matters is that unschooled children have people around them who provide learning models by the way they live, in the activities they pursue. However much parents may desire that their child learn to enjoy reading, that child will be unlikely to do so if she never sees her parents reading for pleasure. If the adults in the family are not obviously curious about and interested in the world they live in, if they never ask questions and search out answers, if they never try things just to see what happens, their kids will seldom do so either.

For most unschooling parents, learning becomes something they do along with their children. Sometimes the entire family gets caught up in some topic, often for extended periods. Often the kids will be intrigued with something they see their parents doing and get involved themselves, but almost as often the parents are drawn into unexpected topics by one or more of the kids.

> However much parents may desire that their child learn to enjoy reading, that child will be unlikely to do so if she never sees her parents reading for pleasure.

I view integrating my children into my life as important. Learning the nitty-gritty of running a household, errands, chores, laundry, meals—all are grist for the mill. The qualities needed? Love for your children, delight in watching them grow, a desire to spend lots of time with them, a willingness to search for an answer and to say "I don't know," the willingness to learn alongside them, even things that you might not have pursued without their good example. —*Carol B.,* Florida

Nobody believes it is as easy as it is. Live your life with your children, include them, and help them find answers to their questions. Many unschooling parents refer to themselves as facilitators. I especially love this word because of its relationship to "facile." Breathing takes effort, too, but we don't concentrate thought on it. —*Cindy,* Wisconsin

What's crucial is the desire to learn. And the entire unschooling philosophy hangs on that objective: find, nourish, and protect a child's desire to learn. You can jointly experiment with *how,* as long as the child wants to, but when the child loses interest and you have to struggle to get any attention and focus, the effort needed to get a result is several orders of magnitude greater, and it's not clear that the results stick. Worse, the process seems to poison the well, and kids are turned off to other material even before you get to it, because it's being forced on them. —*Patrick,* California

You need to have parents who are active learners as role models for their kids. Many people seem to think it takes all my time. Actually, it takes very little of my time. I mean, on the one hand, it takes all of it, since things are always happening. But I don't have to focus all my time on the kids; I don't have to be right there doing things with them all day. Most of what they do I hear about, but they do it on their own. —*Linda,* New York

There are, of course, plenty of times when the parents' role is more overt and deliberate. Anyone who has ever spent time with a preschooler knows how many questions kids can ask, and unschooled kids tend to keep asking those questions as they grow. Unschooling parents have to expect to hear hundreds and thousands of questions, and they have to be prepared to either answer or to help find answers when they don't know. (And they should expect to demonstrate *often* how much they don't know!)

You need to *not* be bugged by kids' questions, and you need to be able to answer them. You especially need to be able to say "I don't know" and "Let's go look it up." You need to be able to *not* teach, and just see yourself as a facilitator of learning. My daughter's glare when I slip into teacher mode shuts me up pretty fast. I have to remember it's my job to "strew her path with interesting things." (That's a quote I stole from Sandra Dodd on America Online, by the way.) —*Joyce*, Massachusetts

> Unschooling parents have to expect to hear hundreds and thousands of questions, and they have to be prepared either to answer or to help find answers when they don't know. (And they should expect to demonstrate *often* how much they don't know!)

Unschooling doesn't mean waiting for him to discover everything on his own at all. I feel there are a lot of things we want him to know about, and certain things he's going to need to know about. This has never been a problem. We respect him and he respects us. He understands that we know a lot about living in the world, and he goes along with our ideas about what knowledge is good to pursue. He also has his own interests which he is free to pursue and which we support in any way we can. I've found his pursuits always to be valuable in leading him to more and more tangents and useful skills. We do a lot of learning together, and I think this is a much more natural way of life than the school model. —*Lillian*, California

Trust That the Child Will Learn

For many people, this last characteristic—trusting that the child will learn—is one of the most difficult hurdles to understanding how unschooling works. "But how do you know you are covering everything important?" "How do you know your kids aren't missing some crucial topic?" "What if they don't learn all the stuff they're supposed to know?"

This is partly a reaction to our own educational experiences and our observations of school children. Years in school teach most of us to rely on what the experts—teachers, textbook writers, standardized test developers, government officials—tell us we need to know. Eager, hand-waving "Me, me, call on *me!*" first-graders become less enthusiastic—even indifferent—by the time they are ten or eleven. Too many times, they are told to settle down, wait until next period, until tomorrow, until next year, we'll cover that later. It doesn't take more than two or three years for kids to quit exhibiting their natural curiosity, to learn to wait more or less patiently—if uninterestedly— to be told what the next "important" thing to learn will be.

Developing the trust that kids can and will learn on their own is usually easier for parents who start homeschooling before their children reach school age. It's hard to watch your children learn to walk, learn to understand and use language, and learn to get into anything and everything within reach, without believing that they are capable of learning about anything they are curious about. Most small children have such a broad range of interests that it's easy to believe they may eventually become curious about almost everything.

I am constantly amazed at what Sean knows just because he has been sitting around reading anything that doesn't move for the last eight years. We have many resources here for the kids to browse, use, discard, or ignore. What is interesting to me is what Glynnis is learning right now. She is a nonconfident beginning reader now, but she is obsessed with cars! She follows them closely, knows every make, and is learning more about them by the minute. Also, she loves to play dolls—dolls in dollhouses or baby dolls. Who knows what she is getting from all this?
—*Melissa, California*

> It's hard to watch your children learn to walk, learn to understand and use language, and learn to get into anything and everything within reach, without believing that they are capable of learning about anything they are curious about.

I attended a "free" school as a child, and spent the larger part of four years under tables playing a long, drawn-out role-playing game. I went to school every day and had the freedom there to do whatever I wanted,

which ranged from raising chickens in the basement, to making up recipes in the school kitchen, to writing plays, to learning algebra at the age of ten. I remember more from those four years than I do from the other eight years of school. I *know* it works to allow kids to live their lives. I've been there.
—*Linda,* New York

For families who begin unschooling after their children have attended school, learning to let unschooling work is usually a more difficult process. It can take time—weeks, months, sometimes even years—for children to rediscover their natural curiosity, to adapt to the concept that what and how they learn is up to them, to believe enough in their own abilities to let themselves care deeply about what they do. In her book, *The Teenage Liberation Handbook,* Grace Llewellyn calls this period "The Vacation" and recommends that families explicitly plan to deal with this initial period of adjustment to a way of life without bells and schedules and rules about what to do and when.

The Vacation can be stressful for kids, who sometimes are mystified about what they are "supposed" to be doing and wait in a sort of limbo for their parents to give them a hint or two, but it can be excruciating for parents. All too often, parents leap enthusiastically into unschooling, expecting that their children will immediately invent all sorts of fascinating projects, while those same children happily watch television or videos for hours each day, or spend unbelievably long stretches of time sprawled out on the sofa, napping.

When my daughter was in preschool, I tried small forays into teaching her academic things I felt she needed to know. She rejected them. I despaired of all the things ahead she "needed" to learn; how was I going to teach her? I felt inadequate that I couldn't come up with a fun method for everything. I even considered unit studies, but I tend to go way overboard, not wanting to start until I have everything in place. Then what if she had no interest in my carefully crafted unit on kings and queens?

I was very skeptical that my daughter could learn "everything" through unschooling, but it sounded much easier, and those doing it seemed to be having fun. It took quite a while, but seeing how much my daughter was taking in by following what interested her at the moment finally convinced me. I realized I wasn't going to ruin her for life if we read Greek mythology instead of learning about "our community helpers" in kindergarten. —*Joyce*, Massachusetts

When I took them out [of school] the second time, we had a period of regrouping. I needed to do lots of reading. I hadn't done any before because the homeschooling was supposed to be a temporary fix to a temporary problem. I knew little of the homeschooling world or how versatile it is. So I set out to read and the kids set out to explore. They spent hours at a time out on the trampoline in the backyard, and worked on various projects (all self-imposed) lasting from two days to three weeks. I saw that they were learning on their own and was in awe of what I saw. —*Andrea*, Nevada

I was in school from when I was five and a half until I was eight, but we didn't really start unschooling until I was eleven. My mom was pretty strict the first couple of years, since I did not know how to read when I was pulled out of school. All I remember of the first year was learning how to read and learning how to type. I hated both. I'm really glad I know how to type and read, but I still think I learned before I was ready. We never really had a curriculum, except for spelling. I hated spelling, too, and I still don't consider myself a very good speller; I just memorize the words I use all the time. Mom used to worry in the first two or three years whether Donald and I would learn anything or not, but I think she just needed to learn that we would and that it takes time. Donald still surprises her about being interested in things she never thought he would be interested in. We had to unschool Mom, too. —*Chase*, Florida

Once kids and parents both grasp the idea that learning occurs any time, anywhere, there's usually still that pesky worry about "covering everything you need to know." But even those of us who've unschooled all our children's lives are still constantly surprised at how much our children learn in the course of their normal, everyday activities. We discover that our kids don't need the repetition that so often permeates school instruction, because they are actively pursuing topics that interest them.

> What [Andrea] learns has meaning. I was a good student, and did very well in school. But most of what I learned stuck with me just long enough to be tested. I knew then it was stupid, but it was a game I was good at. What I see happening with Andrea is *real* learning. It's amazing and wonderful, and very different from the "education" I received. —*Stefani,* New Hampshire

But what about all those topics taught in school? Can we really trust that kids will learn social studies and math and language arts and earth science and all those myriad other subjects that they are expected to learn a little about every school year? The answer, of course, is yes, but it's a somewhat complicated yes. The unschooled child will not acquire the exact knowledge that a conventionally schooled counterpart acquires during a given year, nor will she acquire the same knowledge as other unschooled children. But over the course of several years, unschooled kids will indeed learn at least as much as more formally educated students and will often far outstrip them in many areas.

What they learn, though, will not necessarily fall easily into traditional subject categories. Unschooling parents who live where they

must document their children's learning to comply with their state's legal requirements often devote considerable time and ingenuity to translating what their children do into terms that make sense for reports designed for a more conventional approach to education. For example, a child baking bread may easily learn about following directions, measuring, using appropriate tools and equipment, adding and multiplying fractions, yeast and carbon dioxide, grains and gluten and salt, reading temperature settings and timers, heat convection and conduction, and division and subtraction as the bread is consumed. Is this home economics, reading, arithmetic, study skills, biology, chemistry, nutrition, or physics? All of these topics, or only some of them? That they are not explicitly identified at each and every step does not make the knowledge and skills gained any less real.

The categories of knowledge are simply artificial; they exist for reasons that have nothing to do with learning, nor with the advancement of knowledge. Chemistry blends seamlessly into physics and math and biology and sociology, and shortly you find yourself having danced over to literature. Rather than create artificial boundaries, it's fun to see where something leads. And a burning interest in auto mechanics can lead someone to learn to read well (there being an example in my own family of just that). As I see it, children have already learned so much by "school age" that if one simply helps keep that fire alive, they will continue to learn. And if one doesn't define subject matter rigidly, then it becomes very hard for a child to decide that they don't like—or that they fear—math or science or literature. No doubt there will be things they don't care for, or find hard. But they may well find that pieces of something remain interesting and accessible to them—and those are doorways back into the subject at some future time.
—*Patrick*, California

Institutional learning's set curricula were designed to accommodate the challenges and limitations of a system that puts a large number of children of the same age in one room for five or six hours a day, five days a week. There is nothing magic about the subjects that have been chosen for a particular age level that makes it essential to learn them at that time. There is also nothing sacred about the chosen subjects themselves. If we back up and take a clear look at what our children need to learn by the time they are in their teens, we can see that they need to know how to read and to enjoy reading, to speak well, to write coherently, to understand basic mathematical concepts, to know how to find information, to have a passionate interest (or two, or more), and to have skills that give

> **Q: Are there things you do now that you couldn't do if you were in school?**
>
> BEN (9): When I'm not going anywhere tomorrow, I can read very late and then get up later. You learn about what you want to. I think it's a lot better, because if you get really interested you don't have to stop. I've been reading dragon mythology for about a year, and I think it would be a lot better if there were more dragon mythology.

them high self-esteem and confidence in their own abilities. There is no natural timetable but the child's own, just as we've found with following the child's lead in starting solid food, weaning, toilet training, etc.
—*Terry*, British Columbia

Research Support for Unschooling

All these anecdotal accounts sound well and good, but aren't these really just a bunch of proud parents bragging about their own children? Is there any theoretical support for this idea of letting children direct their own learning? Does research into human cognition have anything to say about such an unconventional approach to education?

"Multiple Intelligences" and Learning Styles
Psychologist Howard Gardner argued in his 1983 book, *Frames of Mind*, that human intelligence is not a single unitary property. Instead, he posited the existence of several distinct competences or

intelligences. He suggested, based on his research, that there are at least seven types of intelligence:

1. Linguistic intelligence, having to do with language and its use. Individuals gifted in this area may enjoy playing around with language, with reading and writing, with sounds and meaning and narrative. They are often good spellers and find it easy to remember dates, places, and names.

2. Musical intelligence, having to do with music, rhythm, and pitch. These individuals may be good at making music themselves or may be sensitive to music and melody. Some may concentrate better when music is played; many often sing or hum to themselves.

3. Logical-mathematical intelligence, having to do with patterns, relationships, numbers, and logic. These individuals tend to be good at puzzles, arithmetic, and figuring out solutions to mental problems; they often enjoy computers and programming.

4. Spatial intelligence, having to do with shapes and locations and visualizing the relationships between them. These individuals usually enjoy designing and building, and are good with maps, diagrams, and charts.

5. Bodily-kinesthetic intelligence, having to do with physical movement and skills. These individuals are the dancers and actors, the craftspeople and athletes. They are often mechanically gifted and good at mimicry, and frequently find it difficult to sit still.

6. Interpersonal intelligence, having to do with understanding and dealing with other people. These individuals are often good communicators and organizers, and are very social. They are usually good at understanding the feelings and motives of others.

7. Intrapersonal intelligence, having to do with understanding one's self. These individuals are often self-sufficient, and enjoy pursuing

activities on their own. They tend to be self-confident and opinionated, and choose occupations in which they can exert some control over how they spend their time.

According to Gardner, each of us possesses a combination of these intelligences, and the relative strength of each determines what we are good at and enjoy. Traditionally, schools have emphasized the logical-mathematical and linguistic intelligences to the near-exclusion of the rest. Those of us whose gifts lie within other areas often have a difficult time in conventional school settings, even to the extent of being judged learning-disabled or handicapped in some manner. Even worse, the demands of conventional school may make it difficult or impossible to develop our native talents enough to discover what we are really good at.

Gardner advocates that schools should make a point of offering instruction designed to accommodate all the different intelligences—to recognize the entire range of human intellectual gifts. By allowing individuals to follow their interests and learn in the ways they learn best, unschoolers tend to work from their strengths instead of focusing on their weaknesses.

> By allowing individuals to follow their interests and learn in the ways they learn best, unschoolers tend to work from their strengths instead of focusing on their weaknesses.

Intrinsic Motivation and Autonomy

Conventional schools have traditionally been hotbeds of "operant conditioning"—the idea that students will perform better if they have some sort of reward to look forward to. To those who exhibit the proper behavior, schools are great distributors of goodies: gold stars and stickers, grades, certificates, honor society memberships, and—lately—bumper stickers with which parents can advertise their child's school success. Some businesses offer incentive programs for encouraging academic success (such as Pizza Hut's "Book-It" program, in which students are rewarded with free pizzas for reading books), and a few schools have even experimented with monetary rewards for good grades.

Consider that last idea for a minute: schools encouraging students by offering money as a reward for good grades, which are themselves a reward for doing work that meets specific standards. Doesn't that seem just a bit removed from the actual learning that's supposed to be taking place? Isn't there just a hint there of the belief that learning is not something that any normal individuals would choose to do on their own, for its inherent interest and value?

That's exactly what Alfie Kohn asks in his book, *Punished by Rewards: The Trouble with Gold Stars, Incentive Plans, A's, Praise, and Other Bribes.* Kohn reviews hundreds of studies, not just of children in schools, but of employees in workplaces as well. He contends that, while rewards instituted to influence people's behavior may very well be effective in the short term, with continued use they become less effective for prompting the desired behavior and, in fact, may actually *discourage* that behavior.

What happens, says Kohn, is that reward systems focus attention on the awards instead of on the original task. The student begins to focus on preserving her grade-point average, concentrating on writing the papers and exams that will give her the highest grades instead of on the content of what she studies. Once she receives the desired grade, what she learned is quickly forgotten in the pursuit of the next test, the next paper, the next grade. The worker who seeks a big profit-sharing bonus begins to focus on maximizing immediate sales to the detriment of her customers' satisfaction, which may result in a decline in sales over the long term.

For Kohn, the solution is "intrinsic motivation," allowing individuals to understand the reasons for the requested behavior and to willingly cooperate, using what he calls "the three C's": content, collaboration, and choice. If desired behaviors do not occur, the first step is to look at the content of the behavior: Is it actually a reasonable expectation? Is there some obstacle to its achievement? Exploring the content implies collaboration in looking for the answers and in discovering alternatives; it gives each individual choices about how to behave. In the short run, this process is considerably more complicated and time-consuming than the typical reward system; in the long run, it becomes far easier and more effective.

One of the researchers whose studies Kohn cites is Edward Deci, who has conducted considerable research into self-motivation. Deci says that self-motivation has two essential components: authenticity and autonomy. By authenticity, Deci means that an individual must be acting according to her own true self rather than merely internalizing someone else's values. By autonomy, he means that the individual controls her behavior, deciding what to do and how to behave.

Among the experiments Deci describes in his book, *Why We Do What We Do,* is an elegant example of the effects of intrinsic motivation on the learning process. Two groups of elementary students were asked to do some reading. One group was told that they would be tested on what they read; the other group was given no expectation of any test or evaluation. When both groups were tested, the group that expected the test demonstrated better rote memorization, but the group that had not expected the test showed better understanding of the concepts contained in the reading. Interestingly, the researchers returned a week later and tested the two groups again. As they expected, none of the children remembered as much as they had for the first test. Surprisingly, though, the children who had originally expected to be tested had forgotten far more than the children who'd simply read the material without expecting to be tested.

In study after study—in the home, in schools, in workplaces— the results were similar: people who are allowed to make their own decisions about how they behave perform more competently and more effectively than those whose behavior is strictly controlled and judged by others.

What Unschooling Looks Like

If unschoolers don't do formal lessons or follow specific curricula, how do they spend their time? If we know that parents aren't giving kids assignments and testing them on what they've learned, what does happen? What does an unschooling household look like?

> People who are allowed to make their own decisions about how they behave perform more competently and more effectively than those whose behavior is strictly controlled and judged by others.

One night we were watching a television special on H. G. Wells and his *War of the Worlds*. Ally found this fascinating and began to read the book right after the show ended. It was on a weekend, so technically if we were using a structured approach to homeschooling, I probably would have felt I needed to go through the book, pick out vocabulary words to use for spelling, and create discussion questions, and tell her she couldn't read the book until I had done all this. But because she had the desire to read, she read. If I had told her "we will study this now," I would be ruining good literature for her, not to mention forcing something on her that maybe she wasn't ready for. —*Marianne, Arizona*

If I sat down and tried to get Andrea to work on math problems, she would often block on the simplest things. If we talk about fractions and probability while planning a frog hunt (which we actually did yesterday), she gets enthusiastic and starts making up her own problems. She has very little interest in writing something someone else assigns, but she writes all the time, in many different styles. She is a very natural, skillful writer. Her spelling has improved without my doing anything more than pointing out an error once in a while. She reads very well, but I wouldn't dream of telling her what to read. It just flows. Whenever I think she's not really doing enough

"school" stuff, she usually takes off again on a new interest.
—*Stefani,* New Hampshire

Unschooling is easier than more structured approaches to learning because there is far less formal work required. There are no lessons to plan, no lectures or assignments to give, no tests to write and grade. Unschooling is also more difficult in that everyone is always ready to learn; anything and everything may turn out to be an "educational" activity. Far from "doing nothing," as some critics of unschooling accuse them, unschooling parents are heavily involved with their children's learning. But the process is not one that's imposed on them; it is a highly collaborative process.

Unschooling is also a process that tends to produce individuals with certain characteristics in common:

- To unschoolers, learning is as natural as breathing—as worthwhile for its own sake, something that happens all the time, rather than in a specific place at a specific time according to a set schedule. Curiosity is a constant, not to be denied because the setting is not overtly educational or the topic does not fall into a familiar school category.

- Unschoolers realize that different people learn different subjects at different times; they tend not to judge individuals based on how "smart" they are or what grade they're in. A group of homeschooled kids will assume that not every seven-year-old reads yet but that some are great fort-builders; most will naturally make allowances in their play for the widely differing skill levels.

- Unschoolers tend to be less peer-centered in their ideas and activities, and more interested in and tolerant of a wide variety of people. Generally, they are more willing to play with both younger and older children, and welcome adult friendships as well.

- Unschoolers tend to have a good sense of self—of confidence in their own ability to learn, to figure things out for themselves. In unfamiliar circumstances, they are willing and able to ask for help and guidance.

- Unschoolers, because they learn how to evaluate ideas from a variety of sources, are usually less likely to automatically accept someone else's word as fact. They are critical thinkers who look for consistency and sense in what they hear and read.

We'll spend the rest of this book exploring how and why unschoolers become successful learners.

Resources

Books

Armstrong, Thomas. *In Their Own Way: Discovering and Encouraging Your Child's Personal Learning Style* (J. P. Tarcher, 1987). Using Gardner's theory of multiple intelligences, Armstrong offers concrete and practical ideas for discovering and working with your children's learning styles.

Armstrong, Thomas. *Seven Kinds of Smart: Identifying and Developing Your Many Intelligences* (Plume, 1993). Armstrong offers exercises and tests for identifying and developing the different intelligences.

Deci, Edward L. *Why We Do What We Do: Understanding Self-Motivation* (Penguin, 1996). Despite its clunky psychological jargon, Deci's book is a fascinating look at how our reasons for doing things affect our abilities.

Gardner, Howard. *Frames of Mind: The Theory of Multiple Intelligences* (Basic Books, 1993). Gardner's exposition of his multiple intelligences theory is interesting reading, if not as accessible and downright practical as Armstrong's popularizations.

Gatto, John Taylor. *Dumbing Us Down: The Hidden Curriculum of Compulsory Education* (New Society Publishers, 1991). Former New York State Teacher of the Year, Gatto is scathing in his assessment of conventional education; his description of how libraries differ from schools is classic and a favorite of many unschoolers.

Hern, Matt. *Deschooling Our Lives* (New Society Publishers, 1996). Hern's collection of essays offers a look at alternative education and homeschooling from a variety of viewpoints.

Holt, John. *Learning All the Time* (Addison-Wesley, 1990). Holt's last book discusses how children learn without being taught.

Kohn, Alfie. *No Contest: The Case Against Competition* (Houghton Mifflin, 1992). Kohn argues that competition is not the natural motivator we often assume it is, and that it often keeps us from doing our best.

Kohn, Alfie. *Punished by Rewards: The Trouble with Gold Stars, Incentive Plans, A's, Praise, and Other Bribes* (Houghton Mifflin, 1995). Kohn argues convincingly that rewards are a system of controlling people's behavior and are only temporarily effective.

Llewellyn, Grace. *The Teenage Liberation Handbook: How to Quit School and Get a Real Life and Education* (Lowry House, 1991). Not only for teens, Llewellyn's first book is good for anyone who wants to get excited about life and learning, with thorough coverage of the ideas of unschooling, plus lots of resources to get started on a variety of subjects.

Llewellyn, Grace. *Real Lives: Eleven Teenagers Who Don't Go to School* (Lowry House, 1993). A sequel of sorts to *The Teenage Liberation Handbook, Real Lives* is a riveting collection of essays by teens about their unschooling lives.

Llewellyn, Grace. *Freedom Challenge: African-American Homeschoolers* (Lowry House, 1996). This collection of essays by African-American and multiracial families about their unschooling lives would be of interest to anyone considering unschooling.

Magazines

Growing Without Schooling (2269 Massachusetts Avenue, Cambridge, MA 02140; 617-864-3100; bimonthly, $25/year) was founded by John Holt in 1977. The magazine concentrates, as always, on stories from its readers about how their children learn. Interviews, book and resource reviews, and other news items are also included.

Home Education Magazine (P.O. Box 587, Palmer, AK 99645; 907-746-1336; e-mail: HEM-info@home-ed-magazine.com; www.home-ed-magazine.com; bi-monthly, $24/year) is more broadly focused than *Growing Without Schooling*, providing more news of alternative education and the politics of homeschooling.

Internet Resources

Online Mailing Lists

The Home Ed List does not specifically focus on unschooling, but it often contains discussions of issues relevant to unschoolers. Home Ed is available as a regular mailing list and in two digest forms (unabridged and abridged, with all the jokes and flame wars deleted). To subscribe to the regular list, send an e-mail containing the message "subscribe" to home-ed-request@world.std.com; to subscribe to one of the digests, send an e-mail message containing either "subscribe abridged home-ed-digest" or "subscribe unabridged home-ed-digest" to dm@world.std.com.

The Unschooling List focuses specifically on unschooling, and is generally a friendly and supportive list. To subscribe, send either "subscribe unschooling-list" or "subscribe unschooling-list-digest" to majordomo@ctel.net.

The Radical Unschooling List is a relatively new addition to the group, formed in 1997 when a few hard-core Unschooling List subscribers decided they wanted a forum that concentrated solely on child-led learning, where no one talked about phonics or math workbooks. To subscribe, send either "subscribe ru" or "subscribe ru-digest" to majordomo@serv1.ncte.org.

Web Sites

Jon's Homeschool Resource Page (http://www.midnightbeach.com/hs/) is low on fancy graphics, but has long been and will probably remain one of the most complete homeschooling sites on the Web. Jon's got huge lists of resources, both online and off, and links to just about everything. One of the best parts is the "FAQs and Essays" page, with an interesting collection of some of the best writing available on the Web about unschooling. And, unlike many Web site creators, Jon regularly checks his links to make sure they still work. If you can't find a recommended resource any other way, check Jon's page; if it's out there, he's probably got a working link to it.

Heather's Homeschooling Page (http://www.madrone.com/home-ed.htm) is where Heather Madrone, one of the longtime regulars of the Home Ed mailing list, has collected some of her favorite posts about learning and unschooling.

Home Education Magazine (www.home-ed-magazine.com) is the Web site for the publishers of *Home Education Magazine.*

Growing Without Schooling (http://www.holtgws.com) maintains a Web site, which includes information about John Holt's Bookstore as well.

AOL Homeschool Connection Home Page (http://members.aol.com/hsconnect/index.htm) is an overview of the very active America Online homeschooling forums, along with the forum e-mail newsletter and the usual resources and links.

CHAPTER TWO

Resources: Finding What You Need

HOMESCHOOLING PARENTS WHO opt for a relatively traditional approach to their children's education have a daunting task ahead of them. They have to decide whether to use a complete commercial curriculum package, to purchase a correspondence program (with or without an advisory teaching service), or to develop their own curriculum tailored to their specific needs. If they choose the package route, they have dozens—even scores—of programs to evaluate. With the custom approach, their choices multiply by the number of topics they decide to cover, and can include many of the same texts and programs commonly used in schools.

The decisions to make can seem endless: Does this algebra book explain concepts clearly enough? Does that literature collection contain selections appropriate for this fourth-grader? Are there enough levels in this spelling book to cover five or six years of spelling lessons? Does that history text cover the necessary material while staying interesting and unbiased?

Unschoolers take a somewhat different approach to learning materials:

Today my children learned by using: a clear plastic bag, tape, the newspaper, scissors, a dozen or more books, two videos, a TV show, cardboard tubes, pens and pencils, tissue paper, a flashlight, cat food, a construction site, several friends, my keys, the telephone, blocks, a train set, a mancala game, an old shoelace, the dictionary, crayons, paper, stickers, a coloring/activity book, a martial arts class, a measuring cup, knives, fruit, the blender, snails, a couple of computer games, bean plants, a swivel chair, baggies, ice, water, the freezer, paper plates, old photographs, a travel brochure, a spray bottle, a plastic fork, cardboard, an egg, french fries, an etymology dictionary, an old alarm clock, a feather duster, me, and probably several hundred other things I didn't even notice. —*Laura D., Texas*

> Most of us are so used to thinking of education as that formal process of lectures, textbooks, exercises, and exams that we forget how much we learn from our surroundings without even thinking about it.

Most of us are so used to thinking of education as that formal process of lectures, textbooks, exercises, and exams that we forget how much we learn from our surroundings without even thinking about it. Infants and toddlers learn concepts of light and dark, shape and color, motion and inertia—hundreds of concepts so obvious that we seldom think of them as having to be learned at all. As they grow older, kids don't suddenly drop this informal style of learning in favor of the more explicit approach; they (and most adults) simply become less aware of it.

What I get a kick out of is seeing how much Ethan learns from what might look to someone from the outside like meaningless games! What adults often don't take the time and attention to see is that kids are learning an enormous amount about computing and a lot of other things with their interest in gaming. My son reads a lot of adult-level books, but he also loves to read through gaming magazines, and takes a great interest in the marketing and advertising strategies at play. He's learning a lot about how ethics affect customer relations and sales, for instance, and he finds it fascinating. It was, in fact, Nintendo Power Strategy Guides that boosted him into real reading, from the Little Bear level to multi-syllable words. I was stunned when I realized he wasn't just looking at the pictures, but actually reading those books. I know of several other boys who had the same experience; they wanted the information out of those magazines, so they really applied themselves to decoding it. —*Lillian,* California

Unschooling families work to remain aware of how much we all learn from what we find around us. Part of this process means that we make sure there are plenty of interesting things around to learn from. Often those things are, as Laura described above, perfectly ordinary everyday items—sometimes used as they are meant to be used, sometimes for other purposes entirely (as when the pots and pans become the percussion section of a family band).

Objects, of course, are not the only educational things around. Younger children, especially, are usually eager to do whatever they see their parents or other adults doing—from routine chores such as cooking, cleaning, and gardening to hobbies and crafts such as quilting, building models, and making music. Working or playing alongside older family members or friends, kids learn not just the specifics of a particular activity, but more general skills and principles: project planning, cooperation, problem solving, time management, budgeting, responsibility, and so on.

Books, Books, and More Books

But parents new to unschooling—as well as veteran unschooling parents who are as vulnerable to worrying as any parents—often worry about how their children can possibly learn everything they "ought" to know without being told exactly what that everything is.

What do you like about unschooling?

SHAUNA (13): I'm able to learn in a nonpressured environment, where the main focus is on preparing for being a part of the adult world. I am the one who decides what I'm going to do each day. My main interests are food and nutrition, math, and reading. So that's what I do. If I were in school, someone else would be controlling my learning, which doesn't make sense. If I were in school, I couldn't read in the tree, with my dog, or in the papasan chair.

How do you help kids learn when the process seems so haphazard and casual? Where do you find the materials you need for those subjects that can't possibly be picked up informally? What do you do when your kids are older and want to learn subjects you know little or nothing about? How do you tell good materials from the rest? Where do you even start?

I browse catalogs, teacher stores, our local homeschool store, science shops, the library, the bookstore. Whatever looks fun or has some good ideas for activities I think the kids would enjoy ends up somewhere on my shelves. I love math manipulatives, because I think they help us explore abstract concepts more easily. We also buy many, many books: children's books, reference books, classics, joke books, anything that strikes us.

I have a few curriculum resources, which we use when the kids ask for something to do, but they are not a regular part of our lives. We take full advantage of our library. Often we use it as the "try before you buy" resource.

I guess I ultimately decide on the resources, but I ask for and receive much input from both the children and my husband. Some days I think I should just buy a case of glue sticks and that would be enough! My entire

criteria are based on what they might like or what they are interested in.
—*Amy*, Idaho

Of course we use a lot of books. We haunt used book stores and garage sales and make frequent use of the discount cards we get from the big book chains. I love the springtime trips to the homeschooling conventions to find the books that you can't see anywhere else. Occasionally I will order recommended books from catalogs. —*Carolyn*, Pennsylvania

I, for one, love to pore over catalogs. There are so many really cool things to promote learning out there. We love books, so there's a lot of literature around the house, as well as technical books. The kids choose from what we have and from what's available at the library. If I like something (like a nature "spotter's guide"), or if I think one of the kids will like it (like Lego Dacta or real watercolor paint), I try hard to get it. Enthusiasm usually spreads around the whole group. I often ask the kids to peruse a catalog and mark the things they like. Even small children can do this.
—*Cathy R.*, Pennsylvania

Homeschoolers are greedy and voracious consumers of books, and unschoolers are no exception. But textbooks are one type of book you're not likely to find a lot of in most unschoolers' homes. (A few unschoolers even take the extreme view that anyone who so much as glances at a textbook cannot be a true unschooler, but most would not go that far.) Unschoolers prefer what we usually call "real" books— books written by and for people who are interested in their subjects, without excessive concern about the level of vocabulary or sentence complexity, whether the book meets state educational guidelines, or how many supplementary workbooks, study guides, and coordinated manipulatives are available.

When I want to know about something, I usually see if they have a children's book in the local library. Children's books are great, because they give you a nice overview of the subject without getting too

technical, and even tell you how to say some of those technical words so you don't sound like an idiot. —*Chase*, Florida

What's important is to find books that answer the questions your kids are asking, and the best way to do that is to make sure they are involved in the entire process. Asking a question is not simply formulating a question and waiting for someone to supply an answer. It's also figuring out what kind of answers are needed, how deeply a subject needs to be explored, whether the first answer leads to new questions and new topics, and how the answers relate to what is already known.

> Asking a question is not simply formulating a question and waiting for someone to supply an answer. It's also figuring out what kind of answers are needed, how deeply a subject needs to be explored, whether the first answer leads to new questions and new topics, and how the answers relate to what is already known.

For example, let's say your nine-year-old daughter asks why a pachycephalosaurus is called a pachycephalosaurus. The fact that the word means "thick-headed dinosaur" may not be enough to answer the question for her. She may be interested in knowing why scientists have come to use so many Greek and Latin word roots to name things instead of simply saying "large thick-headed lizard creature." She may want to know more about the anatomy of this particular creature or how it differs from related species, or perhaps she wants to know when and where and by whom its fossils were first found. It may be that she will not know precisely what she wants to know until she discovers that the first few answers she comes upon are not enough for her. Without being integrally involved in finding her answers, she might never know herself exactly what she's asking.

This means lots of digging around in libraries and bookstores looking for the right information; the younger your children are, the more help they will need from you. To continue with our example, though, dinosaurs are one of those topics for which dozens—even hundreds—of books are available. If paleontology is no particular interest of yours, how do you decide among the myriad resources?

For many of us, this is one of the greatest advantages of the unschooling approach. We are not limited to one or two textbooks that dispense information in "developmentally appropriate" little nuggets. We can cart home a couple dozen books from the library and look at how ideas and knowledge about dinosaurs have changed since people first began to study their fossils seriously. We can learn about the lively debates among paleontologists over the nature of dinosaurs and how they are related to extant animal species. We can observe the huge variety of opinions on what they looked like, what they ate, how they behaved, how they survived for so long, and why they perished. We can read firsthand accounts of research and exploration, and begin to understand that the acquisition of knowledge is seldom as simple as presented in textbooks.

When textbooks are used, they are more likely to be treated as reference volumes, used to find answers to specific problems or as one of numerous sources of information, rather than as a comprehensive, sequential means of mastering a particular body of knowledge. If one text is unsatisfactory, it is easily dropped in favor of a better one.

Anything we put forward either interests them or doesn't. If it's uninteresting, it's not going to be learned, really. Somewhere out there, there is a text, or approach, or idea, that can make that information interesting or worthwhile. And we'd prefer to find that, rather than try to force some unwanted information on a child—because our fundamental objective is to keep alive their love of learning, and desire to learn, and to help them learn to find information they want. —*Patrick*, California

This process of searching and sifting becomes second nature after a few years, and teaches our kids (and us, too, if we have not already learned it!) to think and read critically and skeptically, to evaluate statements in terms of what we already know and what makes sense. It quickly becomes apparent that it's pointless to believe something to be true just because a book or magazine, a television program, or a Web page said so.

Life for unschoolers is easier today than it was even a few years ago, though, because there are more of us sharing our experiences. Instead of having to do all our own digging for every subject that interests our families, we can start with resources that other unschooling families have already found useful. By talking with other families in a local support group, reading reviews in state and national homeschooling newsletters and magazines, and poring over catalogs published by families whose search for resources turned into home-based businesses, we can usually get a good start on finding materials about almost any subject. Other families can tell us what they thought of this particular book for their quiet independent learner, and how that other kit worked with their always physically active seven-year-old. As long as we take recommendations as just that—recommendations—and not as mandatory, suggestions from other unschooling families can be quite useful in finding materials that suit the interests and personalities of our kids.

Other Fun Stuff

Many of the sources from which unschoolers learn are all around us anyway, depending on where and how we live. Naturally enough, families who do a lot of gardening or raise animals tend to have

children who learn a great deal from working and playing in the garden or with the animals. Other families might play games of all kinds—card games, board games, strategy games, word games, puzzles—or spend lots of time volunteering within their communities. Still others make music an important part of their everyday lives.

Most unschooling families keep supplies of paper and craft materials on hand, perhaps with odds and ends of wood and fabric or gadgets like old phones and radios. The mix of "stuff" varies with each family, and it changes within each family as the children grow and their interests change. The drawers of crayons, poster paints, and construction paper give way to sketchbooks and watercolors, and wooden blocks and Brio toys are replaced by Lego and K'Nex sets. In time, all may be replaced by the tools of a serious craft or art.

I'm not nearly omniscient enough to anticipate exactly what my children will use and how they will use it, so I aim for a good supply of arts and crafts materials, odds and ends to create and experiment with, games, music, reference books of all sorts, and friends who know and do interesting things.

Given nothing at all special to play with, my children will still find things. From drinking-straw wrappers to business cards, to rocks, sticks, and window shades, they figure out something to do, and invariably come running to me with a new discovery. I get the wonderful mommy-pleasure of searching out materials and leaving them around for them to find. That first moment of excitement and "Hey, Mom! Look at this!" will always bring a big wide grin to my face. —*Laura D., Texas*

Whatever the specific items turn out to be for your family, maintaining such collections does not have to amount to a major expense. Thrift shops, yard sales, and hand-me-downs from family and friends can provide lots of materials, and local homeschool groups often end up swapping the same resources around for years as members' kids get hooked by and eventually outgrow interest in them.

We've always bought things when we see them cheap, instead of waiting until the kids showed an interest, because you never know if you'll find them again. (We just hope we can remember where they are when we need them.) Musical instruments are a good example of this. We have many, many different instruments, and the kids know they are welcome to mess with them whenever they want. If they show a particular interest, we offer to get them lessons (if we can find someone who knows how to play that instrument). —*Susan*, Iowa

One word of warning, though: It's all too easy to go overboard believing that you need certain items in order to unschool properly. Unschoolers may have an easy time in the homeschool conference vendor hall resisting the twelve different phonics programs and the math software guaranteed to properly drill arithmetic facts into their kids, but often we're just as tempted as our kids by the next interesting-looking kit or fun software package we see, and snap it up before we get around to considering whether it's something we or our kids really need.

> One word of warning, though: It's all too easy to go overboard believing that you need certain items in order to unschool properly.

I bought a ton of stuff which I have only minimally used. I tried to find "gifted" materials, but found that most of them were designed either to keep the kids busy or to teach creativity—something that I wasn't worried about. A classic example was the "Create a Culture" kit I saw. Andrea invented her own culture, the African Fighter Dragons, a few years ago, and devised detailed customs and wrote many stories about them. She didn't need a "kit" to get her started. —*Stefani*, New Hampshire

Learning from People

Inevitably, the day comes when one of your children is fascinated by a topic you know nothing about, and you decide the time has come to seek an outside instructor. It might be music, dance, martial arts, or perhaps something a bit more out of the usual run of kids' classes.

You may well find that locating acceptable teachers for unschooled kids is more difficult than for conventionally schooled kids.

In fields such as ballet or martial arts, where instruction is carefully sequenced to develop physical skills, unschooled kids usually adapt fairly well; it's easy to understand the reasons for the mandated progression. You'll just need to choose the particular style that interests your family.

But other skills can be acquired in more flexible ways. Your unschooled child may have definite ideas about what she wants to learn and how she wants to learn it, and finding a teacher willing to consider and work with those ideas may require more time and effort.

When Elisabeth wanted art classes, she wanted to learn new techniques she could use in executing her own ideas. The first class we found was very product-oriented; instead of using the new technique to draw what she wanted to draw, she was expected to draw the exact same picture as the rest of the students in the class. If they had then been allowed to explore the technique with their own ideas, it would have made some sense, but they just went right on to the next technique and prescribed product. She ended up with lots of little pictures and figurines to give to grandparents, but she almost completely quit drawing on her own. We tried a couple of other instructors, but haven't yet found someone willing to think of a student as a fellow artist looking for new skills. —*Ann*, California

Like other homeschoolers, unschooled kids sometimes have problems with group lessons. All too often, kids are enrolled in classes by their parents because the parents think the lessons would be good for them—or because it gives the kids something to do between the end of the school day and the time when the parents get home. The students who are seriously interested in the content of the class may get frustrated or impatient with the inattention or misbehavior of students who are less focused, and may feel they are not learning all they could be in that setting.

Private lessons may be more satisfactory, but—as with choosing textbooks—it's important to keep your child involved in the process of choosing an instructor or mentor. Your child may not even be able to articulate what she is looking for in an instructor; you'll want someone who is willing and able to help her figure out where she wants to go with her work. Is the instructor willing to listen to your child's ideas? Is your child comfortable with the instructor and willing to listen to her ideas as well? Ask for a trial period to see how things work out, and don't be afraid to look for another person if necessary. The extra trouble will be well worth it in the long run.

Resources

The two books listed here complement each other in their coverage, and are my favorite first resort when looking into an unfamiliar topic. The catalogs are a fairly arbitrary selection among scores available that are popular with many unschooling families. Some catalogs are from home-based businesses that target homeschooling families; others just happen to carry the kinds of materials unschoolers like.

Books

Reed, Donn. *The Home School Source Book* (Brook Farm Books, 1991). Reed's book is part catalog and part collection of essays about learning and living. The catalog portion is a bit more traditionally academic than *Good Stuff* (see next resource), but has longer, more opinionated descriptions of each item. Even if you disagree with Donn's opinions, he's clear enough in what he says that he's often a useful guide anyway. (Note: Donn's widow, Jean, is currently working on a revised edition of the *Source Book*.)

Rupp, Rebecca. *Good Stuff: Learning Tools for All Ages* (Holt Associates, 1997). *Good Stuff* lists all kinds of nontextbook learning materials: games, cards, posters, magazines, books, catalogs, etc., divided by topic.

Catalogs

Chinaberry Book Service, Inc., 2780 Via Orange Way, Spring Valley, CA 91978; 800-776-2242. The Chinaberry catalog is almost as much fun to read as the books it lists, with lengthy descriptions of each title to make any reader (or read-to kid) drool. Titles are divided into sections according to reading level rather than age or grade (parenting books and adult "good reads" are included). Chinaberry also carries a good selection of stories-on-tape, craft items, and a few good games and puzzles.

The Drinking Gourd Book Company, P.O. Box 2557, Redmond, WA 98073; 800-TDG-5487; tdrnknggrd@aol.com. The Drinking Gourd, run by homeschooling mom (and popular homeschool conference speaker) Donna Nichols-White, carries a wide range of books and other tools "for builders, tinkerers, and independent thinkers." It's especially strong in multicultural literature and history, including historical novels and biographies, and in science and math, with a variety of text-type and less formal math and science books, software, and tools, including Lego Dacta sets.

F.U.N. Books, 1688 Bellhaven Woods Court, Pasadena, MD 21122-3727; 410-360-7330; FUNNews@MCImail.com; http://members.aol.com/FUNNews. FUN Books is a good general unschooling catalog, put together by Billy and Nancy Greer, who also publish a newsletter for unschooling families. In addition to a good section about homeschooling and learning, they provide a list of Web sites of interest to unschoolers.

Genius Tribe, P.O. Box 1014, Eugene, OR 97440-1014; 541-686-2315. Genius Tribe ("tools for unschoolers and other free people") is a fascinating catalog put together by Grace Llewellyn, author of *The Teenage Liberation Handbook*. Not surprisingly, its contents are aimed at teens and adults, and include books on independent learning, finding meaningful work, history, philosophy, art, writing, activism, volunteerism, and somewhat unexpected topics, such as belly dancing.

HearthSong, 6519 N. Galena Road, P.O. 1773, Peoria, IL 61656-1773; 800-325-2502. HearthSong's catalog is a lovely collection of Waldorf-based books, toys, crafts, and games most suitable for younger kids, probably eight and under. Their products are not cheap, but they're solid and satisfying—suitable for years of use and handing down to younger siblings and cousins.

Home Again, 1825 North 183rd Street, Seattle, WA 98133; 888-666-0721; www.home-again.com. Home Again offers a line of Waldorf-type crafts and toys, along with books, card and board games, storytelling tapes, and computer software.

Klutz Press, 2121 Staunton Court, Palo Alto, CA 94306; 415-424-0739. This one's pure fun. If you've got kids you're probably familiar with Klutz titles, with their book-and-something-to-fiddle-with format that's inspired dozens of imitators. But you may not be familiar with their Klutz Flying Apparatus Catalog; it is even more fun, and includes professional juggling equipment, unicycles, and other playful items, as well as great books. My favorite is *Watercolor for the Artistically Undiscovered*—the only art book I know of that can make absolutely everyone believe they can really paint.

CHAPTER THREE

TV or Not TV (and Other Questions of Technology)

Technology is a big issue in schools these days. Major corporations donate equipment and personnel to "wire" local schools. TVs and videotape players are commonplace, and even calculators are often considered indispensable classroom tools. But despite all the concern about preparing American youth for a technologically demanding future, there's no real agreement on the place of technology in the classroom, on what tools and skills students need for that future, or on how students should acquire those skills.

Unschoolers, like the rest of our society, have no consensus on the proper place of technology in their children's education. Discussions of technology issues among homeschoolers on the Internet mailing lists are ubiquitous and lively. Rarely do more than a few months pass without another version of the TV dispute, which invariably and rapidly progresses from a calm, intellectual discussion to a vehement and impassioned flamefest. Computers and their appropriate use provoke almost as much debate, although without quite the same degree of fervor.

Television and Video

Unschoolers' views on television fall across the entire spectrum, from no limits at all to no TV at all:

> We own two televisions. One is in the family room and one is in the girls' bedroom to give me a little relief from the noise. Some days the kids watch hours of TV; other days they watch none. In a week I would say they watch around fifteen hours. We have no restrictions on television watching—except volume! I don't feel there is any point to restricting their viewing. I want them to learn to self-regulate, not be dependent on me to tell them what they should do. Also, it would be antithetical to my unschooling philosophy to prescribe or proscribe any source of information. —*Amy,* Idaho

> I loathe most of what's on TV—the advertising and the constant interruptive quality of it. Occasionally, my parents will tape something from an educational channel and pass it on. In my view, the noise-to-signal ratio of TV is so high that what you miss isn't worth the price. There is no TV in this house. The kids can and do watch some at friends' homes, but most of it is parentally filtered. I consider TV to be—overall—the bread and circuses of our age. All the mindless crap you care to wallow in is there, twenty-four hours a day.
>
> Even so, I'll admit that there is educational material on TV—in much the same sense that Soviet history texts contain facts; the problem is finding and identifying it, and not getting caught by the rest of it. —*Patrick,* California

Unschoolers' criticisms of television are much the same as those of society in general. Like many pediatricians and conventional educators, unschooling critics of television recommend severely limiting or completely eliminating TV viewing, on the following grounds:

- Television viewing is passive, demanding neither thought nor interaction.

- Television encourages sedentary behavior, and contributes to children's appalling lack of physical fitness.

- Television is a mediating barrier between the viewer and reality; the viewer sees only what the program's creator chooses to show, and sees even that much only remotely and indirectly.

- Television is a relentless consumer of the viewer's time; almost without noticing it, viewers lose hours of time which would be better spent with books, hobbies, family outings, or other useful and rewarding activities.

- Television glorifies and encourages violence.

- Television offers an unrealistic view of the world, with far too much emphasis on commercialism and consumption—all the worst characteristics of our society.

Many unschooling families, however, believe that television is not an unalterably negative influence on children, and find it a valuable part of children's lives. These families tend to notice that their kids are pretty sensible about their TV watching, and that their use of television differs in several ways from that of the stereotypical TV-addicted child.

They mostly watch PBS; they love *Magic School Bus, Bill Nye, Storytime,* and *Reading Rainbow.* They also have started watching the *Little House* series just this week. It has prompted them to ask for the books, which I have begun reading aloud.

I don't perceive TV as a threat to my children's intellectual development. If anything, it is a benefit. My children learn some things from television that I could never teach them, and other things that it just wouldn't occur to me to teach them. It is an intellectual pursuit, just like everything else in our lives.

I believe their social awareness is enhanced, even if solely because I explain my disagreement with what they tell me. I think they have already learned that we don't have to believe everything we see on television. We discuss ways to evaluate what they see in terms of what they already know. —*Amy*, Idaho

We haven't made any rules. On her own, Andrea has always gone through spells of lots of TV, followed by almost none. She's often more eager to turn it off than we are. She watches a lot of Nickelodeon right now, and I don't object. She gets so many ideas for books from what she sees and has gleaned a rather interesting view of the world (very offbeat sense of humor) from the programs. I am always happy when she's intensely interested in a documentary. It's a form she loves and it's a wonderful way to learn. We all love books, but there is just no comparison when it comes to learning about an ancient civilization, or space exploration, or nature subjects, or almost anything. Being able to see what they are talking about is wonderful.

Many of Andrea's passions have come from TV documentaries, and she watches them over and over. One example was a *Planet of Life* episode called "Ancient Oceans," which spawned several months of intense interest in Cambrian-era life-forms. Usually the video produces enough interest to send her looking for more in books, and then she writes about what she's learning. She wrote several fictional stories about Pterapsis (not your usual main character!). —*Stefani*, New Hampshire

The children and I watch specific programs and rarely remember to turn it on otherwise. In fact, unless we leave Post-It notes on the screen or cabinet, we often forget to turn it on for what we *want* to watch; I can't recall the last time I saw network news. (Although recently we had a week of illness, and we all vegged out on the Cartoon Network, Nick at Nite, Disney, etc.)

On average, I'd guess at least fifty percent of our learning is started, fulfilled, supplemented, or enhanced by television, video-tapes, or computer work. It's my Saturday morning ritual to read the program listings for the coming week and prepare the Post-It notes. The

VCR is used extensively in this regard, and for Friday night movies. Since the kids were toddlers, Friday night has been movie night, with popcorn, soft drinks, and movies 'til they drop. No bedtime; as long as they're awake, we'll keep putting them in. Between purchased and taped movies and shows, I'd guess our video library hovers around two hundred items. —*Jo,* Louisiana

Among unschooling families, one of television's most common uses is as a spark or trigger for further learning. Such families seldom leave the kids to watch television alone; the parents encourage their kids to observe carefully, think, and talk about what they see, and the children often learn a great deal from surprising sources. The kids who enjoy watching *Xena, Warrior Princess* may find themselves fascinated as much by the series' glaring historical and mythological anachronisms as by the show's action sequences. And those action sequences—with their frequent violations of the laws of physics—have been known to prompt serious discussions of gravity, momentum, and inertia (and later experiments with dolls and mini-trampolines).

Every time I try to describe how we do unschooling, I am embarrassed and surprised at how much we use television. And we don't even watch that much. *Hercules* sparked Katherine's interest in Greek mythology. *Linnea in Monet's Garden* sparked her interest in Monet. From *Teenage Mutant Ninja Turtles,* I read to her a bit about the turtles' famous-artist namesakes; *Speed Racer* got us into a discussion of limited versus full animation, a crude demonstration of how animation works, and some books and videos on old cars. The *Animaniacs* have been a treasure trove, branching off into history, geography, and culture. We've watched historical movies and then put tags on her timeline that runs down the hall. And that doesn't even mention shows like *Bill Nye, Magic School Bus, Wishbone,* and *Kratts' Creatures* that she learns from directly. —*Joyce,* Massachusetts

Sometimes I ask my kids to watch something because I consider it part of their education. They usually complain for five minutes and then hang on every word of the rest of the show. (An exception was *Moby Dick,* with

Gregory Peck. We still laugh about how much they hated that one. It has become a family joke. But, by gum, they'll know for the rest of their lives what people are talking about when they hear mention of *Moby Dick*!) I'm a literature lover, so in addition to reading them lots of classical literature, we watch movies made from books, such as *Treasure Island, Jane Eyre, Caddie Woodlawn, Pride and Prejudice, The Three Musketeers, Kidnapped, The Adventures of Robin Hood,* and so on. Jordan is on a Jane Austen kick right now and watches *Persuasion* and *Sense and Sensibility* over and over.
—*Susan,* Iowa

Of course, few unschoolers watch television only for educational purposes. Like most people, they often watch purely for recreational reasons—because they're too tired to read a book, because they occasionally enjoy something silly, because they simply feel like doing something that doesn't take much doing. Though most unschooled kids may develop the habit of not turning on a TV unless there is something they particularly want to watch and turning it off when there's nothing they want to see, there can also be stretches when they simply aren't interested in doing much except watch TV.

Binges of TV-watching long enough to worry parents are especially common among kids who've just started homeschooling or unschooling. Free of schedules imposed by someone else, such kids often need time to get used to the idea of taking responsibility for their own learning. Watching television becomes a way of adjusting to the new freedom, and also perhaps a way of testing how serious their parents are about the whole idea of child-led learning. (Of course, such binges can just as easily take the form of reading every Nancy Drew or Goosebumps book ever published, or spending several hours a day on a skateboard, but those activities don't carry quite the negative associations that obsessions with TV do.)

In any case, such binges rarely last longer than a few weeks or months; letting them run their course usually results in a kid who is bored to tears and eager to find herself something interesting and worthwhile to do. Rather than worrying about the focus of the binge—be it watching TV or listening to music or playing video games—it's probably more valuable to look into the reasons for the binge, to determine whether there is something your child is worrying about.

Sometimes kids are interested in television itself:

> Ethan's gone through comical short periods of being fascinated with old TV shows like *Dragnet, Get Smart, Superman, Mary Tyler Moore,* or cartoons. I always felt he was really learning something from those, too, even though I wasn't always sure what. Then I realized he was learning about age-old issues, just as in the mythology we read together, and about humor. When he was going through his brief, but intense, cartoon period, he was dissecting it all. He would take note of how the background scenery rolled past at certain repetitive intervals, or how the characters would often run off cliffs and fall only when they noticed they were up in the air, and he would enthusiastically imitate different characters. He pointed out all sorts of things I had never thought about. It's important, I feel, to give a child credit for having some innate intelligence about what he's doing. A child isn't fascinated with something for just no reason.—*Lillian*, California

> We have a video camera. Making videos is very useful in understanding other people's filmwork. We have always been interested in how movies and television are made, but the camera has taken us another step. While the camera belongs to the whole family, it has been the boys who have used it ninety-five percent of the time. They were commissioned by committees at our Unitarian Universalist Fellowship to make a video inventory of the building and to film the mortgage-burning—both real tasks, and neither child-oriented. —*Cindy*, Wisconsin

> Few unschoolers watch television only for educational purposes. Like most people, they often watch purely for recreational reasons—because they're too tired to read a book, because they occasionally enjoy something silly, because they simply feel like doing something that doesn't take much doing.

Paying such attention to the method and style of television can be extremely useful, even for those of us who consider ourselves fairly well-educated already. How images and editing are used to manipulate emotion, how news stories provide not-quite-enough real information, and how biases and opinion sneak into "factual" presentations are essential knowledge for any citizen. A child who grows up learning to look critically and observantly at television will find those analytical skills handy for evaluating situations throughout her life.

Computers and the Internet

Opinions among unschoolers about computers and their appropriate use by and with children are nearly as diverse as those on television viewing. Parents who adopt a Waldorf approach to learning may tend to view computers as completely inappropriate for younger children. Others see computers as encouraging the same sorts of passive, sedentary behavior as they believe television does. Unschoolers, though—perhaps even more than most homeschoolers—often tend to be active computer users, and encourage a wide range of computer-related activities with their children. You will notice a definite tilt in favor of computer use in this section—a not unnatural consequence of recruiting contributors for this book exclusively from Internet mailing lists.

> A child who grows up learning to look critically and observantly at television will find those analytical skills handy for evaluating situations throughout her life.

One of unschooling's big advantages is the flexibility and variety of computer activities children can engage in. Unlike all too many schools, where there is but one computer per classroom or a dedicated computer lab limited to an hour or two's use per week, unschooling families can provide almost unlimited access to computers.

Q: Do you like unschooling?

JOHN (8): I like learning this way. I tell Mom what I want to know and we find out about it. I like the Internet and dictionaries and encyclopedia books. I know I have learned something when it is in my head.

Like most other resources unschoolers keep around the house, computers get used by everyone; they're tools for every day, rather than exotic additions to the normal routine.

The children have been at the computer since nursing (which seems to be far more common than I thought or felt at the time!). They just liked seeing the letters appear on the screen in the word processing programs. Frankly, I feel just about anything to do with it is going to teach something—observation skills, critical thinking, logic, etc.

We have the gamut of software—from *Doom* and *Mortal Kombat* to *Reader Rabbit, Math Blaster,* and *Logical Journey of the Zoombinis.* The children don't have limits on the computer; neither their Internet interest nor their skills are yet to the point where that might be a concern. When the *Mortal Kombat* frenzy hits to the point of bloodshot eyes, I advise a brief respite, but they are allowed back on.

Both Rory and Hallie can type pretty well on the computer; Hallie has asked to learn to type "like you" (touch typing), so we found a book on it. Her work on this comes and goes. Rory's spelling has improved dramatically since the beginning of the year, and I believe a large part is due to his writing on the computer to friends and family and seeing the words in book-like print on the screen. He seems to notice that misspelled words just don't look right. I have hopes that the computer will become an even larger part of their learning. —*Jo, Louisiana*

We currently have one computer (about a year old) and would love to get a second one just for the kids' games so there will be less fighting over the computer. Everybody uses the computer, from the two-year-old to me. We have no limits, although we do strongly encourage whoever is using the computer to be aware of other people's needs for it and to share the games by allowing more than one to be in on them. All three are pretty good about this. They interact and assist each other through problems.

I think the computer is another ideal learning resource. Susie, especially, enjoys the freedom and independence of working on the computer. She really dislikes my interference, except for the "Hey, Mom, come and look at this!" kind of stuff.

I spend lots of time on e-mail and a fair amount doing homeschooling research on the Web. None of the children have shown much interest in the Internet yet, although they keep in touch with one great-grandmother through e-mail. —*Amy, Idaho*

Most families use a mix of software—applications such as word processors and graphics programs, and "edutainment" software designed especially for children. While there are plenty of explicitly educational programs available, and most unschooling families with computers certainly use some of them, they are not a major component of most families' computer use. Far preferable to the scores of drill-type programs available are more open-ended software tools. Solving addition and multiplication problems to win a chance to shoot down alien invaders may be fun for a short while, but a good paint program or strategy game is far more engrossing any day.

We have lots of print-shop-type programs—more children's software than any poor family ought to have—and, of course, programs like MS Publisher and MS Office for the grown-ups. We try to keep a variety of new software available for the kids to try. We would rather overshoot and have them wait six months to use a program than give them something that is no challenge. We find that the age range on software is most often useless. I rely on recommendations from home- and unschooling friends for my software choices. —*Amy,* Idaho

We don't use much so-called educational software; too much of that is "workbooks on the screen" for my taste. We have games of all varieties, word processing, programming languages, etc. We have limited Internet access through our library freenet, but honestly, the kids and I don't really want to devote our time surfing the Web at the moment, although we do use it occasionally for specific things. —*Carol,* Florida

For many families, the Internet is a valued part of their educational program, particularly as the kids get older. Internet resources vary from serious reference sites, such as online library catalogs, encyclopedias and dictionaries, and professional journals, to the downright silly, like Web sites bashing current celebrities or tracking root-beer sales in some college basement vending machine.

We have four computers, three of which are networked. We use a local Internet Service Provider (Bruce has been on the board of a group getting a local community network up and running).

Both boys have access to the Internet, but because of maturity differences they have different guidelines. Dan, at twelve, works on his home page, Web-surfs, is on a few low-volume mailing lists, and sends and receives e-mail to and from people he knows. If he sends e-mail to someone he doesn't know personally, he works with a parent on both the sending and reading. These are generally asking questions of someone in a specialized field, such as "What is the pedicel on an ant used for?" on an insect list. Bruce and I are providing spelling and grammar checks more than monitoring. Dan has used software to learn subjects (how to use a video camera, for one); he also plays games, programs, draws, writes, and is learning to manipulate video on the computer.

Ben, at nine, sends and receives e-mail from friends he knows otherwise and Web-surfs, but may not up- or download without a parent present. He loves educational games and writes stories on his own, but dictates e-mail messages when asking questions of people he hasn't met in person.

The computer is the only area in which we have ever had to insist on a time quota. We have a limit of two hours per day per boy, and the hours must be separated by some real activity. Reading a book or watching a video does not qualify; biking, building a Lego car, or talking with friends does. —*Cindy,* Wisconsin

We all use the computers. No limits, but there is often too much computer time when other kids are over, so I sometimes make a pest of myself and nudge them outside. We live on a country lane, so it feels unhealthy to be clustered around an electronic thing when there's so much wide-open nature to enjoy outside.

We all use the Internet and we all have modems. We use an Internet service provider and connect with America Online through the ISP as well. Our son has full access, and we've had no reason to lay down any rules. There are some seedy things I hope he never comes across online, but we're raising him with good values, so I don't worry much about it. —*Lillian,* California

We have several computers, but of course everyone likes Mom's best. We own a wide variety of educational software and a few games.

Although we are on the Internet as a family, I have found my eldest, at seven, can click on anything and get anywhere very quickly. I am not comfortable with him being on the Internet alone because of this. He can be on the Internet, but only if I am in the room with him.

I really like the availability of this amount of information at our fingertips. So many other homeschoolers don't have computers or aren't on the Internet yet, and I am constantly looking stuff up for them. For those of us out in the boonies, with small libraries, it is much easier to sign on to the

Internet than to drive to a big library somewhere in hopes that they will have the information you want. —*Kathy*, Illinois

I'm not a censoring type of person. I believe in moderation and have tried to instill a sense of this in my children. They are going to be on their own before I know it, and if they don't learn to make their own decisions before they leave home, I've failed in my job. Yes, we have a computer at home and, no, I don't limit how much time they can spend on it, except for making sure that everyone who wants to gets a turn. We are not hooked up to the Internet yet, but when we are I think we'll still be all right. My kids are extremely honest and above-board. I really don't think they would ever sneak around and do things they felt were wrong. I don't worry about this. I expect the Internet to be a resource they will use a lot. —*Susan*, Iowa

> It's best to think of the Internet not as a single, unitary resource, but as what it really is: a vast collection of wildly disparate items, some valuable and some worthless, some harmless and some potentially dangerous.

The Internet can be a great source of answers for all those kid-questions that pop up when the library is closed or when your own library has nothing to offer, but it is by no means perfect. Searching for information can be frustratingly slow, and search engines may not categorize topics in the way most useful to your search. And once you find information, there is no guarantee that it's either current or accurate.

It's best to think of the Internet not as a single, unitary resource, but as what it really is: a vast collection of wildly disparate items, some valuable and some worthless, some harmless and some potentially dangerous. It's easy, though, to overestimate the dangers. If you teach your children to use the same sensible precautions on the Internet that they use with any strange or unknown people or situations, and keep yourself aware of their Internet activities, they'll probably encounter nothing they can't handle.

Resources

Hazen, Don, and Julie Winokur. *We the Media: A Citizen's Guide to Fighting for Media Democracy* (The New Press, 1997). Fascinating overview of the modern media, its corporate interconnections, and the implications for media content, including broadcast and print news and commentary, books, advertising, and more.

Mander, Jerry. *Four Arguments for the Elimination of Television* (William Morrow & Company, 1978). Mander's book about the problems inherent in the very nature of television is a classic criticism of the medium.

Papert, Seymour. *The Children's Machine: Rethinking School in the Age of Computers* (Basic Books, 1994). Papert, who invented the LOGO programming language, is an advocate of open-ended computer activities for children rather than the "drill and kill" approach, and presents ideas bound to interest unschooling families.

Papert, Seymour. *The Connected Family: Bridging the Digital Generation Gap* (Longstreet Press, 1996). Papert's most recent book about children learning with computers is aimed at parents with no computer knowledge whatsoever. This one's a bit commercial as well; the book comes with a CD-ROM containing demo versions of children's software Papert's company has developed.

Perelman, Lewis J. *School's Out: Hyperlearning, the New Technology, and the End of Education* (Avon Books, 1993). Perelman is an enthusiastic advocate of computers for learning, believing they have the potential to utterly transform American education. He's great fun to read, if a bit too breathless from time to time.

Stoll, Clifford. *Silicon Snake Oil: Second Thoughts on the Information Highway* (Anchor Books, 1996). Stoll, an Internet pioneer, questions whether the Internet is as useful or valuable as the hype would have us believe; Stoll's are interesting ideas from a "do as I say, not as I do" point of view.

Winn, Marie. *The Plug-In Drug: Television, Children, and the Family* (Viking Press, 1985). Winn's book is a classic on why television is bad for children and for the family as a whole.

CHAPTER FOUR

How Can You Tell They're Learning?

UNSCHOOLING SKEPTICS ASK the question frequently, almost as often as parents who are starting to consider an unschooling approach for their family: How can you tell they're learning?

For those of us who've been at it for years, the answer seems obvious—hardly worth thinking about. We see our kids every day, talk with them, answer their questions, help them with their projects, watch them help us with our own projects. We see how much more they understand and do than they could the month before or the year before.

How do I know he's learning? I can never help but be stunned by the question. It's so obvious, day in and day out, that he's learning about a lot of things, and that he already knows more than an awful lot of well-educated adults about many subjects. It would be ridiculous to question it. I see how much he reads, how much he discusses ideas and knowledge he's picked up in one way or another. I'd be a darn fool to question whether he's learning. —*Lillian, California*

Being actively involved with the children tells me what they are learning—but I have to think about it. It's kind of like their physical growth. Sure, we know they're growing, but we live with and see them every day. It's kind of hard to tell what's going on until they try to put on that outfit that fit perfectly just a couple of months ago. Now the sleeves are too short, the buttons are being pulled, and the hem is a couple of inches too high. "Boy, have you grown," I exclaim, having really known all along, just not having thought about it. I'm confident they're learning, know they're learning, but am amazed every once in a while with an "I didn't know they knew that!" —*Jo, Louisiana*

Yesterday, our two-and-a-half-year-old said something that was not quite comprehensible while we were driving; it being near bedtime, I gave one of those nondescript responses. He had a fit. When I got him to repeat himself, he asked me, pointing at the car clock, "What do those letters say?" I answered him, and he was happy (and fell asleep a couple of minutes later). What this showed me was that he's fully cognizant that letters go together and make words, and say things. In other words, he's grasped that speech can be written down.

I don't see the basic idea changing as the kids are older. You can ask them questions or get them to help with something that will show a skill. And you pay attention to what they do and say.

Observation and attention.

No, it's not "objective standards"—but then I have grave doubts about "objective," and I'm even more dubious about the idea that people need to fit many standards. I see too great a difference in how individuals learn and what they're interested in to justify fitting them all into Procrustes' bed, at least beyond some very basic skills. Even there, all I want to see is that they achieve mastery of the skills, not that they master them in a specific manner. —*Patrick, California*

Boy, would I love to do school at home and see those textbooks and worksheets piling up! It would be a satisfying physical meter of what's going on. It is very frustrating not to have some tangible way of measuring—

something to calm my fears that she's not learning. But I've had to rely on the way she responds to things, how she approaches a problem. I've also gained confidence by seeing the connections she makes between disparate pieces of information, saying things like, "Oh, that's like in the book we read." The way she answers my questions and the remarks she comes up with all on her own help me. It's just confidence built up from success. It's not something that could have been handed to me at the beginning.
—Joyce, Massachusetts

Rare is the unschooling parent who doesn't occasionally worry about whether their kids are learning enough to eventually become competent, self-supporting adults. It might be a news story about the new computer lab at the local school or the local kid who wins a major scholarship that triggers concern, or it might be noticing that other seven-year-old unschooled kids in your local group are reading chapter books while yours is still struggling with picture books. Even though we know our kids are doing just fine, we sometimes feel that we ought to be able to "prove" it to others, and worry that we might not be able to.

It's not only parents doing the worrying, though; it's fairly common for unschooled kids to also fret about whether they're "keeping up" with their schooled peers. Lacking the stacks of worksheets and test papers of those peers, unschooled kids sometimes feel they spend their time "doing nothing," and begin to wish for an easy way to see that what they know and do is in any way comparable to what school students know and do.

The answer may be as easy as explaining to your kids that different schools teach different topics at different grades and that comparing who knows what when is a rather silly exercise, and pointing out that they have some skills that schoolkids haven't yet developed.

> Rare is the unschooling parent who doesn't occasionally worry about whether their kids are learning enough to eventually become competent, self-supporting adults.

Taking tests every couple of weeks to verify what they've learned won't really tell them anything they don't already know. Some families are quite comfortable with this informal level of evaluation and don't feel any need for more formal records.

We do no formal evaluation or documentation. Of course, we all evaluate things about ourselves and each other every day. Jordan is in the business of making friendship bracelets, which she sells at her dad's antiques shop. She decides each time she finishes one whether it is pretty or not and how much she will ask for it. She might ask my opinion of her work, but she doesn't think in terms of grades or rewards for what she does.

Caleb was a late reader. I have an idea of what grade level he currently reads at; he knows that he has a more difficult time reading than most of the other people he knows, but he certainly doesn't think of himself as a failure. He figures his friends know some things he doesn't know, and he knows some things they don't know. —*Susan,* Iowa

I can tell just by being with my kids that they're learning. Are they learning everything? No, but there's time. There are some things first-graders in school learned that we didn't cover this year; other stuff (lots more, in fact) that we did that school didn't even get close to covering.

I don't put a lot of stock in testing of any kind; it becomes intellectual regurgitation. I keep some formal records. They consist mostly of a notebook along with samples of art projects. I do have trouble breaking things down into subjects sometimes. —*Terri,* Colorado

Keeping Records

Most unschooling families end up keeping some sort of learning records, but the volume and style of such records varies with the reasons for keeping them. You may even decide to keep more than one set of records for each child, since the information required by state law may be entirely different from what you and your children want for your own use. Whether you keep information for your own use, for your children to have something to look back on, for future school and job applications, or for complying with your state's legal requirements, your records will probably take one or more of the following forms.

Narrative Journal

Many families, especially those with younger children, start out with a notebook in which they more or less regularly record learning activities, skills, books read, notable events, and so on.

> Until this year, I kept a running log of what was being done. That is, I tried to record something almost daily. This year the volume is way down, and I've resorted to monthly lists of what's happened (as much as I can remember). It seems like there is so much going on that I hate to take the time to record it all. —*Stefani,* New Hampshire

As Stefani notes, keeping a journal can be time-consuming, to the point where you discourage your kids from doing anything new until you've finished logging the previous activities. Over time, most families tend toward weekly or monthly entries instead of daily entries—and record only more important activities, without any wealth of detail.

Subject/Schedule Grid

Some families choose a grid format for their logs, with academic subjects along one axis and the days of the week along the other. Activities are noted with a few short words or phrases in the appropriate boxes on the grid. Public and private school homeschooling programs often supply (and require) such grids for their enrolled families; they are an easy way to ensure that each curriculum area is covered, and they provide enough information for the supervising teacher to maintain official records.

Q: Do you like unschooling?

CALEB (14): I love it. This is the best. This is just as good as life gets. I like it too much almost. I like that we get our own choice. I've never wished I was in school or regretted that I don't go to school. I think kids are crazy for wanting to go to school.

JORDAN (11): Unschooling is a very good idea. There's not very much pressure on me to get things done. I feel I can really open up and learn. I really like it. When you're not being pushed to learn, you kind of push yourself to learn.

Q: Are there things you wish you could do as an unschooler that you can't? Or things you do now that you couldn't if you were in school?

CALEB: If I was in school I couldn't do all the field trips I do.

Q: What field trips?

CALEB: Going places with Dad.

JORDAN: I feel like I'm missing out on their field trips and missing out on what they're doing. If I went to school I'd be more like schoolkids and not so odd.

CALEB: I don't feel like that at all. I think I'm more popular because I'm unschooled.

JORDAN: If I was in school I couldn't see nature firsthand. I'd be stuck in school looking at pictures. I'd be looking at pictures of animals instead of seeing them firsthand.

The one real difficulty with keeping a grid is breaking activities down into the supplied categories: Should the overnight stay at the working historical farm count as history, as biology, as physical education? Can you mark the same activity down for two or three different categories? Almost any way you decide ends up seeming artificial and contrived; the grid, while relatively easy to do, can be frustratingly incomplete.

We keep the records required by the state, which are completely irrelevant and unrelated to what we really do. They want separate subjects, with activities and "attitudes and skills taught" duly recorded in each subject. I wing it. I put whatever comes to mind in each category. I don't lie, but I make no effort to be very accurate or complete, because the school doesn't want to know what we do. I tried that once; they sent it back and asked me not to do that. So I don't do it anymore. It takes about fifteen or twenty minutes to write these reports for both kids, but I *hate* doing it, because it is so entirely meaningless. —*Linda*, New York

Portfolio

The portfolio is one of the most popular documentation options with homeschoolers. Essentially a glorified scrapbook, a portfolio is a collection of artifacts of the learning process. Drawings, paintings, other artwork, stories, letters to pen pals, journals, computer programs, garden records, science projects, 4-H project records—anything can go into a portfolio. Like the grid (and often in combination with it), the portfolio is popular with school-supervised homeschooling programs.

We see a school-district teacher roughly once a month. The school district keeps a portfolio. Creating things for the portfolio does take a small amount of our attention, but Katherine likes meeting with the teacher and showing some of the things she has done each month. We have a form divided into the general subjects that activities for each subject are recorded in—anything from a field trip to videos or TV shows to books to projects might be noted there, and that is put in the portfolio, along with several examples of her work each month. We might also take screen shots of computer programs she's run. I am fairly relaxed and do not record every book read, and often only record the most notable educational activities. —*Grace, California*

In states where formal record-keeping is not required, the portfolio is an ideal vehicle for keeping work samples. You or your children simply choose which pieces to let serve as examples of the kind of work done over the period of the portfolio; whether you choose to include explanatory notes or a specific number of certain types of items is entirely up to you.

I keep projects they have completed (at least photographs of them, anyway—some are pretty big!), paintings, worksheets they have chosen to do, poems they have written, etc., all in files. Each child has his own color-coded file in my file drawer. I stick stuff in as I clean up. Once a year it gets sorted out, and the stuff we decide to save goes in an envelope marked with their name and age. That envelope goes into a box I keep in my closet. —*Kathy, Illinois*

Transcripts
Traditional transcripts, with course titles, credit hours, and letter grades, are not used much by unschooling families. This is partly due

Paul's Transcript

Paul homeschooled until the age of fifteen, when he began to take classes at the junior college in combination with homeschooling. Our philosophy of homeschooling integrates education and life, so although Paul has strong skills and abilities, he does not have a traditional high-school transcript. The skills and abilities Paul acquired during his education are listed below.

MATH ABILITY

- Paul taught himself algebra, geometry, trigonometry, and calculus using a variety of textbooks. He was placed in second-semester calculus at [the junior college].

- He is proficient in programming in Pascal, C, C++, HTML, and Java. As a volunteer, he helps maintain a state organization's Web site.

- He developed a 3-D engine in C++. He performed the necessary math calculations, created 3-D transformation and 3-D translation routines, and programmed a depth-sort algorithm.

WRITING ABILITY

- Paul has written computer-game reviews professionally for [a nationally distributed computer magazine] since he was fifteen.

- He participated in our homeschooling writing club for four years.

- He co-edits the bimonthly newsletter for a statewide organization.

- Currently, he is working on an independent research/writing project with a professor of genetics.

(continues)

READING ABILITY

- At present, most of Paul's reading consists of computer manuals, programming books, and science and math books.

- He has read widely in a variety of genres, including classics, science fiction, and biographies.

SCIENTIFIC KNOWLEDGE

- Paul was fascinated with natural history as a young child, and collected boxes of rocks and strange pets for many years.

- He studied baseball and statistics for many years.

- The Physical Science Survey class at [the junior college] introduced him to physics, astronomy, and geology.

- He participated in a homeschool chemistry lab and a genetics lab. He has visited NASA, Lawrence Livermore Lab, and similar science centers.

- He is studying college chemistry at [the junior college].

- He is currently reading Feynman's third book of physics lectures, a book on genetic algorithms, and D'Arcy Thompson's *On Growth and Form*.

KNOWLEDGE OF THE WORLD

- Paul has traveled widely in the U.S. and Canada with his family and on his own. He traveled across the country several times, stopping at various parks and historical sites, and staying with homeschooling families. He ferried to Alaska and drove back with his family. He has camped all over the West. He lived in a small town in New England for many weeks and spent a summer in a remote town in Washington.

- Paul learned geography, history, and social studies through reading, computer games, various field trips, and discussion.

FOREIGN LANGUAGE

- Paul completed two semesters of American Sign Language at [the junior college].

FINE ARTS

- Paul played in a French horn choir for many years.

- He has drawn for years; he designed and drew his own series of baseball cards when he was younger. He studied drawing at [the junior college].

- He volunteered to participate in a community recycling event in costume as Roscoe the Steel Can.

SELF-DIRECTION AND INITIATIVE

- Paul challenges himself with programming problems to solve. He thinks a problem through, tries a solution, refines the solution, and only then researches how others have solved that problem. That is how he taught himself to program.

- Paul is able to create a study plan for himself and complete it. He is studying college chemistry this semester without having completed the high school chemistry prerequisite. The teacher thought he was unprepared for the class, but he convinced her to let him try it. In four weeks, he memorized the periodic table, learned a year of high school chemistry, and earned an "A" on the first midterm.

CRITICAL THINKING ABILITY

- Paul helps others with their programming problems.

- He plays strategy games for fun, has won Magic card tournaments, and excels at logic problems and visual spatial problems.

(continues)

- Paul taught himself advanced mathematics using textbooks and references, and then using his skills in computer programming.

- He enjoys the mental exercise of problem solving.

ABILITY TO WORK IN A GROUP

- For the last five years, Paul and several friends worked as a team to build a vehicle for the Tech Challenge competition at the Tech Museum of Innovation. The team succeeded in designing and operating successful vehicles using found objects, recycled materials, and/or inexpensive materials.

- He attended several courses through Pathfinders: a ropes course, a leadership course, white-water rafting, and canoeing.

- He won the team spirit award three years in a row at baseball camp.

PHYSICAL EDUCATION

- Paul regularly bikes, walks, works out, plays racquetball, and takes advantage of any opportunity for outdoor fun. He enjoys backpacking, rock climbing, canoeing, and swimming. He will play baseball or basketball when given the opportunity.

LOVE OF LEARNING

- Paul is a dedicated and creative student. He studies with the expectation of fully learning and understanding the material.

- When visiting a prospective campus recently, Paul spent an hour in the bookstore reviewing and choosing books on biological computer modeling, genetic algorithms, and neural science. He was thrilled to find a bookstore that catered to his interests and intellect.

to the difficulty of translating learner-led experiences into traditional course outlines. While a child may learn most of the content of a conventional United States history course by the time she is fifteen or sixteen, she does not necessarily learn that material in chronological order, in any one year, or in a number of hours that converts easily to the Carnegie units schools are familiar with. Trying to force the individualized educations of unschoolers into conventional transcripts is usually more trouble than it's worth.

That said, some unschoolers do take the trouble to create a transcript, either because they are more comfortable presenting themselves with a traditional-looking transcript, or because they must deal with an institution (employer, college, or the armed forces) that simply isn't prepared to deal with an unconventional portfolio. One way unschoolers can present their educational history for college and job applications is shown in the sidebar entitled "Paul's Transcript." Other methods for presenting such information are described in some of the books in the resource list at the end of this chapter.

Testing

As you may have guessed by now, most unschoolers take a rather jaundiced view of testing, whether it is the normal everyday variety, aimed at gauging student grasp of specific course material, or the increasingly common standardized tests now given in even the youngest grades. (We'll talk about college admissions testing in Chapter 10.)

In general, unschoolers view tests as irrelevant to their lives and learning. Parents already have a good idea of their children's skills and knowledge simply from spending as much time with them as they do, so the everyday sort of tests seem mostly a waste of time. In states where periodic standardized tests are mandated, unschooled children tend to do, on average, as well as or better than conventionally schooled students, without any more special

preparation than a quick review of filling in answer-sheet bubbles with #2 pencils.

But many unschoolers also have philosophical objections to standardized tests:

I think the results of the tests my husband and I took in school were damaging to relationships with parents, siblings, teachers, and friends. I tested very high. He tested flat average. We were treated accordingly, and we would have been better treated as ourselves instead of as our scores. I don't want that for my children. I don't want them graded and scored and measured and labeled. I will resist it as far as I can. —*Sandra*, New Mexico

All too often, the results of standardized tests create expectations—either positive or negative—that children are expected to live up to. A child who does poorly on such a test may suddenly find that she is not expected to accomplish much, even though her entire history until that test belies the result. Conversely, one who does well may suddenly have to live with unrealistic expectations of "genius" or "gifted," whatever those terms may mean. Most of us prefer to look at our children as their whole selves—as what they are and what they do—rather than as statistics distilled from a morning's selection of multiple-choice test items.

Some Examples

In real life, of course, most unschooling families use a combination of means to keep track of what they learn; they do not rely solely on any single method. And whatever means they use changes with the ages and needs of their children. Above all, as the children get older and take more responsibility for their own learning, they will probably take much of the responsibility for maintaining their own records as well.

The particular mix of tools each family adopts depends on the styles and personalities of the parents and the kids, on the types of activities they choose, and on the laws regulating homeschooling in their state. The following three examples—from Florida, Wisconsin, and Pennsylvania—give some idea of the variation and flexibility inherent in the whole process.

The best way of telling that my kids are learning is to listen to them talk. Unfortunately, Florida requires annual evaluations until age sixteen. In my mind, I don't draw a line between things being educational or not; everything is "life." We have chosen to use Clonlara [a private school that offers services to unschoolers] for two reasons: to give the kids a "real" diploma so they won't have to spend their lives explaining what we did (unless they want to!), and to handle the annual evaluation, because Donald is essentially untestable. We use the portfolio review and assessment by a Florida certified teacher. I keep an informal journal (list of books, programs, activities) for each month and a grid to check off covered subject areas for the state records for Donald. Lynda keeps time sheets for her credits for Clonlara—and dislikes it! I would probably keep the informal journal just for us, even if nothing was required, but would chuck the rest if I could. I often have trouble deciding what to record and how to break it down into subject categories—such arbitrary divisions! —*Carol,* Florida

My training was in science, and scientists are big on record-keeping. The laboratory notebook crossed with an expanded "baby book" with a dash of calendar would best describe what I do in a Daytimer-type notebook.

Our state requires an attendance record, but we are free to define the school calendar. Ours is 365–366 days long and is kept on a checkbook-sized calendar. Should all of us be down with the flu, I might cross the day off as an absence. Otherwise, a weekend at the cousins' house is certainly a learning time. Trips are probably the most heavily educational time.

And that sitting-around-not-working-on-anything time is a learning time, too. It was my record book that showed me this. After major projects are done, or after a busy holiday season, or just because, there are these long periods of nothing. ("Long" changes definition over time; it has been days or weeks, but seldom more than three weeks.) I sit closer to the edge of my chair and fret more the longer this goes on. Yet every time, there is an eruption of learning activity when they come out of these stretches. I would never have noticed the pattern without my records. It's as if there was a period of digesting a large lump of learning, a need to reflect and assimilate all that knowledge. And when I reflect on myself, I, too, do projects at varying rates. Some may be steady, some more like marathons.

My records have changed over time as my concerns have changed. In the first two years, I was concerned about having to prove that we had spent time learning; our state says that we will have at least 875 hours of instruction. So for the first year, I counted to the nearest five minutes every activity that would qualify as an on-task activity in a more conventional school setting: time spent being read to, time at the library, time investigating how bulldozers are put together, etc., but not time learning to get along with friends or building with Lego. It was arbitrary and I knew it.

I totaled the times each day and kept a running weekly total. Our 875 hours of on-task activities were completed from September to January. We didn't include time spent taking attendance, having recess, passing out papers, or waiting for someone to be quiet. The following year, I was more relaxed and kept times only to the nearest fifteen minutes. We were again done in January. And we never stopped learning just because the 875 hours were used up. For a while, after the times were "complete" I stopped keeping records, but I found that because we were still learning, the records were still helpful.

Today, I never mark times on-task. And not feeling the need to define learning in school terms has made me feel freer to see the connections between designing paper airplanes, baking a Native American cranberry cake, and reading Norse mythology, as well as how all three are but a piece of becoming an ethical and considerate person. —*Cindy*, Wisconsin

This is probably the area in which we unschoolers feel the most uncomfortable. I have conflicting standards. I spend part of my time worrying about whether the children are at grade level, conforming to society's expectations, and demonstrating "sustained progress," as Pennsylvania law requires of us. I spend the other part of my time trying to decide what I really think they should know and how to measure that. Our state law requires annual evaluation by an approved evaluator who interviews the children and examines a portfolio of their work. We also take standardized tests periodically. This keeps the first fears mostly at bay. The other question of what I really think they should be learning is much more important and difficult to assess. I want them to learn to learn, to learn to love, and to learn to love learning. Unfortunately, it's difficult to tell if this is coming about. Unschooling often feels like a big gamble, because you don't know the outcome until you no longer have the responsibility.

We are required by law to keep a daily attendance log for 180 days and a list of books used in our "school." I expand this log to a few sentences about the types of learning we do each day. My log might say, "Consumer math (shopping), wrote a letter, read *Anne of Green Gables,* discussed local history and geography (field trip to local historical site), and discussed personal hygiene (explained why she had to wash her hair)." I do this to give the officials an idea of how unschooling works and to supplement our portfolio because it does not have the usual worksheets, essays, and science journals in it. Our portfolio does contain copies of letters the children have written, tickets from concerts they have attended, souvenirs from trips we have taken, artwork, and photos of the children building K'nex projects, working on the computer, and skiing. The children really enjoy having these records at the end of the year, but the logs and portfolios require persistent effort, and sometimes I resent having to justify our activities to an institution that I don't particularly respect. I spend only five to ten minutes per day per child on logging, but by the 103rd day or so, I get quite weary of it. Sometimes it's very difficult to interpret your children's experiences into the type of academic accomplishments that the school will want to hear about. I also have to spend several hours at the end of the year creating each portfolio. I hope that, as the children get older, they will be able to assume some of these duties.
—*Carolyn,* Pennsylvania

Resources

Cohen, Cafi. *And What About College?* (Holt Associates, 1997). This book is aimed at homeschoolers seeking college admission, but Cohen's method of creating a conventional transcript from a relatively unconventional educational history could also be useful to parents of younger unschoolers.

Colfax, David and Micki. *Hard Times in Paradise* (Warner Books, 1992). Included in this account of the Colfaxes' approach to learning—mostly on their Mendocino County ranch—are descriptions and samples of the process the family used to document learning for themselves and for their (successful) Harvard applications.

Gould, Stephen Jay. *The Mismeasure of Man* (W.W. Norton & Co., 1981). Gould takes a thoroughly fascinating look at the history of intelligence testing and the scientific principles (or lack thereof) behind it. If you're not already skeptical of standardized testing, by the time you finish *Mismeasure of Man*, you will be.

National Center for Fair and Open Testing (FairTest), 342 Broadway, Cambridge, MA 02139-1802; 617-864-4810; FairTest@aol.com. FairTest offers a number of publications on testing and assessment issues, including *Standardized Tests and Our Children*, a thirty-two-page booklet covering basic information about testing, how tests are used and misused, and what you can do about it.

An Unschooling Week One

Since she lives in Pennsylvania, which requires (among other things) "a log, made contemporaneously with the instruction" of homeschoolers' educational activities, Carolyn keeps records for each of her children. Here is a typical week from the third-grade log for her daughter.

DAY 55:

- Learned to bind needlepoint bookmark and almost finished it.

- Learned to do basketball layups.

- Met veterinarian at Brownies and heard presentation.

- Played State to State game and counted all the states that had beaches on major bodies of water.

- Read from *Yukon Ho,* by Bill Watterson.

- Practiced German songs and pronunciation with older friend.

- Listened to friend's flute practice.

- Weighed different Halloween candy bars and calculated "fair" distribution of candy for dessert. Sorted candy into nut and non-nut varieties.

- Discussed percentage and percentile in relation to her standardized test scores.

- Was read to from *Little Town on the Prairie,* by Laura Ingalls Wilder.

(continues)

DAY 56:

- Made fancy hamburger cookies.

- Finished needlepoint bookmark.

- Read *Magic School Bus in the Time of the Dinosaurs*.

- Read *Magic School Bus Baked in a Cake*.

- Read *Yukon Ho*.

- Mailed package at Post Office by herself, paying for postage and counting change.

- Swam for one hour.

- Taught herself to play "Deck the Halls" on the piano.

DAY 57:

- Visited zoo. Explained tracking exhibits to Dad. Observed new river dolphin for extended time.

- Sang in German choir and had concert (four songs).

- Read another American Girl book.

- Did extra chores.

- Started letter to friend.

- Listened to *Yukon Ho*.

- Played piano.

DAY 58:

- Started letter to another friend.

- Finished letter started yesterday.

- Raked leaves.

- Played piano.

DAY 59:

- Journal entry.

- Composed song about our dog.

- Wrote letter to grandfather, wrapped package, and made a fancy homemade birthday card.

- Played Rodent's Revenge and Canfield (strategy games) on computer.

- Assisted Allen with spelling words.

- Read *Happy Hollisters at the Circus.*

- Assisted with dinner.

DAY 60:

- Journal entry.

- Cleaned and set up bird feeder.

- Played outside in first snow.

CHAPTER FIVE

Reading and Writing

L IKE EIGHTY PERCENT of my fellow Baby Boomers, I was taught to read in school with Dick and Jane. The readers we learned from were filled with colorful pictures of Dick, Jane, Sally, Spot, Puff, and their whole gang, busy with their daily adventures. That incredibly stilted, easily parodied, limited-vocabulary text is still difficult to forget:

Look.

Look, look.

Oh, oh, oh.

Oh, oh.

Oh, look.

As first-graders, we had no knowledge of the controversy over the "whole-word" or "look-say" method of reading instruction, which emphasizes the meaning and shape of entire words over the rules for decoding letter sounds. We had no idea that Rudolf Flesch, in his 1955 book *Why Johnny Can't Read,* railed against the very concept of whole-word instruction and advocated phonics instruction as the only hope for America's future.

Even then, though, the battle was an old one:

> When you show a child an object, a dress for instance, has it ever occurred to you to show him separately first the frills, then the sleeves, after that the front, the pockets, the buttons, etc.? No, of course not; you show him the whole and say to him: this is a dress. That is how children learn to speak from their nurses; why not do the same when teaching them to read? Hide from them all ABCs and all the manuals of French and Latin; entertain them with whole words which they can understand and remember with far more ease and pleasure than all the printed letters and syllables. —*Nicholas Adam,* A Trustworthy Method of Learning Any Language Whatsoever, *1787*

Today the pendulum still swings—ever more violently and ever more often—as we sift through all the dogma. Advocates of "whole language" tell us that reading real books with interesting content will motivate kids to become good and enthusiastic readers—that mechanical skills such as spelling and grammar will come with time. Phonics advocates insist that children need basic decoding skills to start with—that good literature will mean nothing if children do not first learn the basics. "Invented spelling" allows children to express ideas beyond their rudimentary skills, say some; as those skills develop, so naturally will their spelling conform to the norm. No, say others, children should get into the habit of writing words correctly from the beginning, so that proper habits become second nature.

Since reading and writing began to be considered universal mandatory skills, the debate has raged between those who believe that children learn them best by emphasizing meaning and understanding first, and those who believe in constructing reading and writing from the smaller building blocks of phonemes and syllables. The remarkable aspect of the entire argument, as it has affected American education, is that each faction is determined that their own way is the One True Way for each and every child to become a competent, literate citizen.

Unschoolers opt for noncombatant status in the language wars. With our natural emphasis on truly individualized learning, we observe the ways our children learn best, and help them pick and choose from among the many available tools to find the ones that work best for them. For most of us, helping our children learn to use language is an utterly pragmatic, undogmatic matter: whatever works is what we—or more properly, they—use.

In this chapter we'll look separately at learning to read and learning to write, but keep in mind that the two are closely linked; children do not learn one without learning about the other. The separation is arbitrary, purely for ease of discussion.

> Helping our children learn to use language is an utterly pragmatic, undogmatic matter: whatever works is what we—or more properly, they—use.

Reading

Reading is the first big, scary learning hurdle for unschoolers. All the debate about reading instruction and all the talk about what an inadequate job our schools do to encourage literacy lead us to believe that learning to read is a difficult, mysterious process that requires professional guidance. In fact, as mysterious a process as reading itself is (any competent reader can only marvel at how easily symbols on paper can transport us to other worlds and other times), learning to read can be far more simple and painless than we expect.

One of the first principles that unschooling parents discover is that there is no standard age at which children naturally learn to read. If allowed to learn at their own pace, some children will read on their own as early as three or four; others will not become fluent, independent readers until they are nine or ten, or even older. In general, though, the pattern they follow in learning to read is pretty much the same no matter what their ages or how long the process takes—anywhere from a few months to several years.

First comes an interest in letters and logos and other symbols, and the realization that wherever they appear—in books and magazines, on television, on roadside signs—they have meaning. Gradually, the child learns to recognize and read such words and symbols, and to associate them with their meanings. The child asks—seemingly constantly, at times—about letter sounds and word pronunciations, and listens attentively, often following along with the text, to stories read to her. She adopts one or two favorite stories or books to be read over and over again, often memorizing the text well enough to fool her parents into thinking she is actually reading. Then, one day, she truly *is* reading for herself. Once the child reaches this stage of reading independently, her reading speed and comprehension progress rapidly; within a few weeks or months, she can (and often does!) read almost any text she comes across.

> One of the first principles that unschooling parents discover is that there is no standard age at which children naturally learn to read. If allowed to learn at their own pace, some children will read on their own as early as three or four; others will not become fluent, independent readers until they are nine or ten, or even older.

I suppose that since I am a compulsive reader—the type who reads cereal boxes and ketchup bottles if there's nothing else around—it was inevitable that I would have a couple of late readers. Both girls started recognizing signs and letters at around four, but neither starting reading on her

own for years. Elisabeth suddenly started reading books for herself a couple of months after her eighth birthday, and Lynne is almost at that point now at nearly nine-and-a-half. Both love books and reading, though, and I'm convinced that Elisabeth, now a voracious reader, would dislike and avoid it if she had been pushed to read earlier. She's always resisted showing her skills publicly until she has perfected them privately to her own satisfaction. Lynne is much more vocal about learning to read than her older sister was; she's full of questions and actively trying to become a better reader.
—*Ann*, California

Susie began truly reading just before she turned six. We thought that was a little late, considering that her father and I both read at age four. I worried a little, realizing that it was ludicrous. She has just started reading for pleasure the last month or so. It has been terrifically rewarding to see her do that—I guess because pleasure reading has been such a vital part of my life. She reads to her younger sisters, and we all read together for at least thirty minutes a day. She loves to read headlines while we read newspapers and magazines, and many times while I read a novel, she cuddles up and announces page headings and initial sentences to me. —*Amy*, Idaho

Whatever other tools you may introduce, the first requirement is one exemplified by this five-step reading program that occasionally appears on homeschooling lists on the Internet:

1. Read to them.
2. Read to them.
3. Read to them.
4. Read to them.
5. Read to them.

It's one of the basic tenets of the whole language approach to literacy: children will not learn to appreciate reading if they never see it being used. Reading aloud will do more to turn your kids into readers than any other single thing you can do. Reading aloud can be a daily event for the entire family, it can be private time for one parent-child pair, or older children can read to younger ones. Many families continue to read aloud together, long after all the children have learned to read, simply because they have come to enjoy the ritual of sharing books.

Susie is our only true reader, at six. In my short-term "curriculum" phase, I bought a highly recommended phonics program. She hated it, naturally. So we just read to them all the time. They see us reading for pleasure and for study, so I'm sure that has an impact. I guess I use some phonics, like when they ask, "Mom, what sound does 'P' make?" but the phonics approach, just like any "approach," didn't work here. My kids are good at memorizing, and I think they just memorize what words look like, as I did at that age. We haven't done any of the little games, like putting name cards on objects around the house like my mother suggested. The girls find such things too contrived, and I agree. —*Amy, Idaho*

We have always read to our children and continue to do so, even now, as a fun family activity. I think this has contributed to their desire to learn to read.

My daughter learned to read at age six in public school, with a combination of phonics and whole language. Now, at ten, she reads fiction constantly for pleasure, but loves it when I read to her. I am the one who tends to read the literature to her, and she tends to read the lighter stuff, over and over again.

My son taught himself to read at age four because he wanted to read things like signs and instructions on the computer. We read to him, provided him with books, and allowed him to plaster signs all over the house, and he did the rest. He seems to know what works for him. He's the one who requires the closed captioning to be turned on when we watch TV, and I think he's learned a lot from that. He doesn't read much, but he reads very difficult material when it's needed to accomplish his goals.
—*Carolyn, Pennsylvania*

How much assistance each child wants or needs varies enormously. What seems to be important is for parents to provide plenty of support: answering all those questions about letters and sounds, playing word games, offering comparisons between new words and ones they already know. For most unschooling families, this sort of wordplay is not a conscious exercise they deliberately work into a certain number of hours every day; it's a natural effect of sharing their pleasure in using and enjoying language.

Sometimes it seems like Jackson was born knowing how to read. He was obsessed with figuring it out from a very early age. We read a lot, played around with words, answered his questions, and talked and listened endlessly, and somehow he put it all together. There was no method at all, other than responding to what he asked for or seemed to need. There were books and stories he wanted to hear a hundred times, computer games he played until he fell asleep on the trackball, videos he memorized and acted out, and the constant rhyming, alliteration, and other linguistic silliness we all engage in.

> Reading aloud will do more to turn your kids into readers than any other single thing you can do.

Now Jackson reads for pleasure, and will read to Sarah for hours at night in bed. She is going about learning to read very differently, motivated as much by wanting to be grown-up as by wanting to know what the words say. She, too, loves rhymes, and lately will ask me to make lists of simple rhyming words for her to read. We haven't felt the need to use any reading programs, or to hurry either child. —*Laura D., Texas*

When I look more closely at their learning, I see that we have played prereading games from the time they could talk. These just came as naturally to us as playing tic-tac-toe to pass the time while sitting in a waiting room. I always had a tablet of paper in my purse for these emergencies, and would draw little pictures and letters and words for pencil games. We also had foam letters that stick to the side of the bathtub when wet. If they had not been having fun with this as play, it would not have been pushed. As it was, this kind of play—and rhyming songs, and lots and lots of reading aloud—added up to children who were ready to leap into reading by the age of five. —*Terry,* British Columbia

We read to Sean from the time he was two weeks old (embarrassing but true; I just couldn't wait to read to him!). When he was four and five, he had memorized many books. At six, we did some real basic phonics with him and he just started reading. He is not really a phonetic reader, but rather a sight reader. We read less to Collin, and he learned to read pho-netically at eight. Glynnis is quite the beginning reader at nine-and-a-half; phonics makes no sense to her! She told me the other day that reading makes her go cross-eyed. Poor Wells, at the tail end, is probably going to end up teaching himself to read.

All the kids love to be read to or listen to stories. Sean reads to live and lives to read; Collin reads for pleasure but has a harder time with things. He really has to love a book to stick with it. He doesn't enjoy the transport of a good story as much as Sean and I do, and won't wait for a good tale un-less it starts well. —*Melissa,* California

When my four-year-old spelled my name ("CAFE") on the refrigerator door with magnetic letters, I realized he was ready to learn some of the rules to "break the code." Very gently, and at their own pace, I have led the kids through some very basic generalities (I hesitate to call them "rules") of phonics, and helped them find books they could read for themselves. This was enough for the oldest, but Mary Elayne required further help with words. She seems to enjoy learning the rules; I think it helps her find her way.— *Cathy R.,* Pennsylvania

I have one avid reader who learned to read at four. He would ask what a word was, and I would answer. He never really understood phonics, al-though I tried to explain some of the basics of it to him. He was (and still is) very much a sight-word reader. He can sound words out, but with many of the more difficult words he is now encountering, phonics do not help. He is now seven and chooses to read several hours a day. He enjoys both fiction and nonfiction and has a reading level around seventh or eighth grade, according to what he has been able to read to me out of books marked with their reading levels.

My youngest is just learning to read now. He is five and has been asking me to teach him. He also does not like phonics, but is finding it does have its uses while he puzzles out a few new sight words. He has a small word deck; each word he knows or has asked to learn I put on a card for him. We have enough cards now that he is beginning to read small sentences.
—*Kathy*, Illinois

While I was worrying about Caleb's difficulties with reading, Jordan learned to read on her own. If anything, I actually encouraged her to wait because I didn't want her to learn before Caleb did and then he'd feel bad. She was definitely a whole language reader. She never had a bit of help other than being read to, being surrounded by reading material, and seeing other people reading. She still reads above grade level and has never had a single lesson of any kind. Caleb has resented her ease of learning to read, but he doesn't hesitate to ask for her help when he needs something read. He knows he's better at other things than she is, so I don't think he worries about it too much. That said, I also know he would ab-solutely love it if reading were easy for him—I guess in the same way that I would love it if running were easy for me. I know I could become a runner if I just made myself run, but I guess I don't want it badly enough to work at

it. Caleb knows he gets better at reading when he reads, but he doesn't want to work at it. He doesn't make me run, so I don't force him to read. I encourage lots and lots, though.

My kids don't check out piles of books from the library or read nov-els for pleasure, but they read a lot. Caleb reads his *Star Wars* cards all day some days, they both read lots of *Tintin* and *Garfield* and other comics-style books, they read instructions on how to do things, and both of them will still listen to me read anything out loud—and I mean anything, from Dr. Seuss to graduate textbooks. They love books, and that's what's really important to me. There's a poster I've seen: "Those who don't read are no better than those who can't." Even if Caleb has trouble with reading, he believes reading is a good thing and understands that good things come from reading. I'm happy about that. —*Susan*, Iowa

Unschooled children seem to derive enormous confidence from learning to read this way—at their own pace, with their own methods. Reading is a skill they have developed for themselves; having mastered one of the most crucial and useful tools for further learning, they are unlikely to believe that many subjects or skills will be too difficult to attempt.

Writing

For many unschooling parents who remember school "language arts"—spelling, penmanship, grammar, composition—with dread, it's something of a shock to find one's children becoming prolific storytellers, correspondents, and calligraphers. For all too many of us, our writing instruction emphasized the mechanics to the near-exclusion of actually having something to say.

Young children learn to write along with learning to read. They begin to grasp the idea of words as labels for things, and they demand to know the labels for their favorites: their own name, names of family members, toys, everyday objects. Alphabet blocks and magnetic letters are favorite toys; they delight in arranging letters in "words" for their parents to pronounce, and are especially tickled with our attempts to pronounce particularly consonant-laden examples.

With writing, our eldest started asking first about words on a page (What word is "train"?), and then wanted to write his name. Then he started playing with letters and was delighted to find that he could create words that we would recognize and read to him. Then he wanted to write a note to his grandparents, or to me when I was away one evening past his bedtime. —*Patrick*, California

Q: How do you spend your time?

CALEB (14): I guess I spend time, well . . . I try to do good things. When the weather's nice I like to play outside. I go with my dad a lot of places and work with him helping outside. I play with my friends when they get home from school. Sometimes I spend days looking at and reading my *Star Wars* cards or comic books or catalogs of science stuff, and then I don't do that again for a while.

JORDAN (11): I try to get outside as much as I can. I jump rope or blow bubbles. I like to plan what I'm going to do in the future. I read lots. Sometimes books and sometimes comic books. I go places with my dad.

Q: How do you decide what to do?

JORDAN: I do what I need to do to be more intelligent. If I think I need to work on cursive, I work on cursive.

CALEB (laughing out loud): She does!

Q: What do you learn the most from?

CALEB: I learn a lot from computers. I also learn from nature and my friends.

JORDAN: I learn most from nature and books. I learn from Dad how to do neat things—like if I ever got lost, I'd know what to do.

Q: How do you know when you've learned something?

CALEB: When I'm with my dad and somebody (an adult) wants to know something and I tell them, that feels really good. It happens a lot.

DAD (laughing out loud): It really does.

JORDAN: I don't know what that means. I just know. I just . . . I just know. I feel happy about what I've learned and that helps me to remember it.

Susie was always very interested in writing the letters. She could write quite legibly before she turned four. I was convinced that she was on the road to reading, but it turned out to be an artistic exercise instead. Susie is now writing cards and signs and posters and things like that all the time. Sarah, at four, is not yet interested. Emily, two, leaves little papers covered with what is supposed to be writing all over the house. (I remember the others doing that, too.) Today Emily discovered the word-processing programs and had a ball making letters appear on the page. —*Amy, Idaho*

I used to tell Andrea the sounds of the letters from when she was tiny. She had those magnetic letters and some plastic letters with animals on them. She began writing on the Magnadoodle, which I think was a good tool. I should emphasize that we didn't push her at any point. She was just very happy learning always—very proud of herself. Her invented spelling was a hoot. I don't really remember correcting it very much (probably not at all early on). She has asked for spellings only occasionally. It seems to be widely variable, but constantly gets better. I think the large amount of read-ing she does is responsible.

She did reverse some letters for a couple of years. She wrote poetry and stories. Almost all of her stories have been imitative, based on what she was reading at the time. Her very first books involved a large number of pregnant mares, which was her obsession at the time. The Redwall series [by Brian Jacques] had a *huge* influence on her writing. She wrote many many Redwall-inspired books. She wrote very little nonfiction until recently, when she began to keep notebooks about subjects of interest, such as na-ture (frogs, salamanders, birds) or the cats. She loves to write; she gets a great deal of satisfaction from her writing and always reads it to me several times as she's working. Right now she's working on a parody of teen maga-zines, only it's for cats. She's taking pictures of all the male cats she can find for an article on cat "hunks" to put in the magazine.

I believe that just providing models of good writing is sufficient to keep her improving. She seems to have always had a good ear for language, and has always been drawn to well-written books. We have always read to her a lot; I can't imagine not doing that. —*Stefani,* New Hampshire

As Stefani mentions, children often reverse and confuse letters—b's and d's, p's and q's—when they first begin to write. In most cases, this is because they concentrate first on the actual shape of the let-ters, only beginning to notice their orientation as they become more proficient. Most children grow out of this very quickly; only rarely does it become a problem.

Reading and writing seemed to come along naturally together. Mary Elayne reversed many letters and numbers, and still does occasionally as an eight-year-old. My opinion is that she felt compelled to learn to read to keep up with her older brother and really should have waited. She's had trouble remembering left and right as well. I think she's made the mistake often enough to doubt herself, and then she's more likely to make the mis-take again. We rarely even mention it, and I'm hoping that she'll gain the confidence she needs. —*Cathy R.,* Pennsylvania

One issue that often arises when unschoolers talk about writing is that of penmanship. A parent laments, "My daughter cannot write!" and immediately is offered advice on projects to interest her in writing: pen pals, postcard exchanges, recording family jokes, and so on. Only when the avalanche of suggestions slows does she get a chance to explain that the problem is not composition but that the girl's illegible penmanship is completely hopeless.

Most unschooling parents are inclined to let our kids' handwriting develop with their fine motor skills. The six-year-old who has difficulty even forming basic letter shapes often draws elaborately decorated letters by the time she is eight or nine. Even the worst penmanship is easy for a child to correct once they are old enough to want to make their writing more legible, and quite a few unschoolers eventually take to experimenting with calligraphy as an art form.

Lynda had trouble with penmanship for years until she decided to work on it with a calligraphy-style italics program. She never finished that book, but she has a pretty hand now when she wants to. As for creative writing, she resisted that for a while until she decided to earn some extra Girl Scout badges that required reports. Now she writes all the time: journals, letters, poetry, short stories, occasional reports that she chooses to do. I read only what she chooses to share, probably less than ten percent of what she does. —*Carol*, Florida

My son seems to be learning to write on his own now at seven. His handwriting is terrible, but he types quite rapidly. He enjoys being humorous and writes silly letters and notes to the whole family. His grandfather just gave him an old electric typewriter, and he spends hours typing little stories, poems, and signs for his room. He also uses the word processor, of course, and actually seems to be learning to spell from the spellchecker. —*Carolyn*, Pennsylvania

Writing and composition are something that Ethan's able to do, but has little interest in. I got him a little hand-held spellchecker to keep by his paper when he writes. He has discovered that if he types things at the computer first, he can concentrate on what he's trying to say instead of having his mind split between composition, spelling, grammar, and handwriting. So he's been typing things up on the word processor first and then copying them in longhand for the handwriting practice. —*Lillian*, California

Most unschooling parents tend to downplay what concerns they have about penmanship and other mechanics of expression in order to encourage their children with its content. Like me, they remember yearning for a magic machine that would take my dictation and produce a perfectly spelled, perfectly scribed composition in my own handwriting—anything to avoid having to recopy those four paragraphs over three times until I successfully produced a clean enough (no more than three errors) version to turn in at school. It's no wonder so many of us learned to write as little as we could get away with.

In consequence, many of us become scribes to our younger children, writing down their stories for them on paper, allowing them to concentrate on what they want to say instead of on whether they are saying it correctly. It's easy to write your child's sentences on the bottom half of a sheet and let her illustrate her story herself later. You can staple the pages into a construction-paper cover to make a small book she can read for herself whenever she wishes. Over time, such books get larger and more elaborate, and gradually your child will begin to take over the writing of the text as well.

Both children love to write letters and stories, and so I write for them whenever they ask. We make books, write screenplays, send letters to friends and relatives, and make all manner of surprise gifts—all their ideas. Jackson can print well enough to write simple notes to me, but it is still difficult for him. He is full of inspiration, though, and so he gets plenty of practice writing as he draws and captions, and writes letters to me and his dad, and all the various other things he gets it into his head to do. Writing is much easier for Sarah, and I suspect that by the time she is a fluent reader, she will be a fluid writer as well. —*Laura D.*, Texas

Sean could write when he learned to read, but really didn't come on in that area until a couple of years later. Collin followed the same pattern but is less willing to write. Glynnis loves to write and would rather write than attempt any reading. —*Melissa*, California

My children all seemed to fall into writing at around the age of five. Our oldest loved to write quite early on, but never wrote anything like a book report or essay. She had several pen pals from the age of ten through her teens, and kept volumes of journals. She has a trunk full of these filled-up journals and is still a journal writer. I think it's being able to express herself verbally, and having read and listened to lots of good books, that make her such a good writer, because we never sat down to teach her to write.

Our middle daughter didn't get into writing or spelling until she was eleven. At six, she'd "written" an excellent little book about the Underground Railroad—by dictation. She would sometimes invent only one new sentence in a week; she would just pull out the story to work on when she felt the inspiration and I'd read what she already had and ask her to imagine herself in the story. She'd go off into fantasy for a moment, then burst out with a new sentence or two. I'd type it onto the page, and she'd pull it out and run to show her father—the end of that writing session! She didn't do much more than that until suddenly, when she was eleven, she started writing poetry, and writing it very, very well. If she'd been in school when she was eleven, I feel sure she'd have been in a "special help" class for her writing. Her spelling was like a secret code, and her writing was a large scrawl. When she started school when she was twelve, she tested a year ahead of her age in language arts. Funny, but it bears out my philosophy that when they're ready it will all come together. She just won a scholarship for her writing—at the college level. —*Terry*, British Columbia

For many unschooled children, the computer is an invaluable tool for writing. With a word processor and rudimentary hunt-and-peck keyboard skills, they can let themselves go—everything from playing with letter shapes

and fonts and print sizes, to writing stories and letters, to producing family or neighborhood newspapers or literary magazines. Spell-checkers aid in learning standard spelling as the children become aware of how much more willing readers are to tackle their publications when their spelling approaches current standards.

Outside projects can also lead to improved writing skills:

- Organizations such as 4-H and Scouts often require members to keep records and report on projects they undertake; when the 4-H rabbit project develops into a full-fledged business, the record-keeping and reports improve almost automatically, simply because they are necessary.

- Literary or theatrical productions are often undertaken by homeschool support groups or other community groups; many unschooled kids will participate for the chance to see their work in print or on stage, and will work furiously to polish it to perfection.

- Pen pals—both electronic and by normal mail—are a good way to polish writing skills.

My older daughter's read for years, but seldom wrote at all until she started corresponding with friends by e-mail. Her spelling and grammar aren't perfect yet, but they've improved tremendously, as has her typing, since she started this. What's even better is that she's progressed from sending one- or two-line jokes to more thoughtful messages several paragraphs long, and she's begun to keep a paper journal now as well.
—*Ann, California*

Literary Synergy

As I mentioned at the beginning of this chapter, it's important to realize that reading and writing are inextricably related. As your child begins to read more complex material, she also becomes capable of writing more complex material. And the reading and writing themselves will be intertwined with other subjects she tackles: she'll compare novels with movies and plays; she'll notice the many different styles of writing and learn when each is appropriate; she'll see places where her developing skills are useful and figure out ways to improve those skills. Reading and writing will be such natural components of her life that she'll hardly think of them as "subjects" in and of themselves.

Resources

Bissex, Glenda. *GNYS AT WRK: A Child Learns to Read and Write* (Harvard University Press, 1980). Bissex, using her five-year-old son as her study subject, offers a fascinating case study of how a child learns to read and write. Includes terrific examples of how children use and then progress beyond invented spelling.

Goldberg, Natalie. *Writing Down the Bones: Freeing the Writer Within* (Shambhala Publications, 1986). For those of us who have trouble getting words onto paper, Goldberg's book provides advice and exercises for making the process easier.

Gordon, Karen Elizabeth. *The Deluxe Transitive Vampire: The Ultimate Handbook of Grammar for the Innocent, the Eager, and the Doomed* (Pantheon Books, 1993). Decorated with Gothic illustrations and teeming with equally Gothic examples of usage, Gordon's book is a painless and often hilarious reference to the basics of English grammar and usage.

Kismaric, Carole, and Marvin Heiferman. *Growing Up with Dick and Jane* (HarperCollins, 1996). This large-format book looks at the history of the "whole-word" approach to reading in the context of this century's history. It comes with a sampler story booklet and cutouts of Dick and Jane, for those of us who have forgotten (or missed entirely) what they were like.

Maguel, Alberto. *A History of Reading* (Penguin Books, 1996). This is a treat for anyone who reads for pleasure, covering books and readers from the age of cuneiform to the age of the CD-ROM—from the years when the elite worried that universal reading would destroy the common oral culture and allow everyone to think for themselves, to our own day, when we lament the decline of books in the face of the cathode-ray tube in its various forms.

Sheffer, Susannah. *Writing Because We Love To: Homeschoolers at Work* (Boynton/Cook Heineman, 1992). Sheffer, the editor of *Growing Without Schooling,* describes her correspondence about writing with homeschoolers age ten to fifteen; excellent look at how unschoolers tackle writing seriously.

Silberman, Alene. *Growing Up Writing: Teaching Our Children to Write, Think, and Learn* (Heineman Educational Books, 1989). Silberman's book describes the work of the Bay Area Writing Project and the National Writing Project, which developed a "process" approach to teaching writing, emphasizing content first and then improving and polishing work through successive drafts.

Smith, Frank. *Reading Without Nonsense* (Teachers College Press, 1985).

Smith, Frank. *Insult to Intelligence* (Heineman Educational Books, 1988). Smith is one of the leading proponents of the "whole language" movement, and is worth reading for an accurate description of how whole language is supposed to work (often quite different from the ways schools have attempted to implement it).

Stillman, Peter R. *Families Writing* (Writers Digest Press, 1992).

Stillman, Peter R. *Write Away! A Friendly Guide for Teenage Writers* (Boynton/ Cook Heineman, 1995). Both of Stillman's books are terrific, full of ideas for making writing a natural part of everyday life. They include great ideas for recording family history and lore, and for using writing as a tool for understanding and learning.

Strunk, William, Jr. and E. B. White. *The Elements of Style* (Macmillan, 1995). Now in its third edition, this little classic may be all the grammar book most of us ever need. E. B. White's final chapter, "An Approach to Style (With a List of Reminders)," is some of the best advice around for making writing clear, readable, and to-the-point.

Wooldridge, Susan Goldsmith. *Poemcrazy: Freeing Your Life with Words* (Three Rivers Press, 1996). Wooldridge's book is full of ideas for collecting and playing with words, for creating poetry without fear or self-consciousness.

Zinsser, William. *Writing to Learn* (HarperCollins, 1989).

Zinsser, William. *On Writing Well: An Informal Guide to Writing Nonfiction* (HarperCollins, 1994). Zinsser's books, like Strunk and White's *Elements of Style,* are classic guides to writing clearly, cleanly, and effectively; these are books writers reread frequently to keep themselves reminded of the fundamentals of good writing style.

CHAPTER SIX

Math and Problem-Solving

M ATH" IS A confusing term. Just as with "writing," by which people may mean either the process of composing and communicating an idea, or the mechanics of actually forming the letters and words, or both, it is not often clear exactly what we mean by the term "math." When we say that all children need to learn math, do we mean that all children should know all four arithmetic operations thoroughly, with fractions and decimals as well as integers? Does that "math" we speak of include geometry and trigonometry? What about more general skills—estimation, logic, and the ability to look at charts and statistics and understand what they mean? Just as in the language arts, the battle rages interminably between the "facts and skills" and the "conceptual understanding" crowds.

General fear and discomfort about things related to any form of mathematics lead a good number of unschooling parents to opt for the "we unschool everything *except* math" approach. Such families worry that their children will never learn "enough" math, and will never master basic arithmetic operations or basic consumer skills, unless they are taught them explicitly. "Saxon Math," a series of textbooks that emphasize skills in a repetitive, incremental presentation, is a popular choice among these families. A structured approach such as Saxon's usually produces competence, but seldom any real pleasure or joy in mathematical ideas.

> The more determinedly "un" unschooling families favor an approach to math that emphasizes conceptual understanding over simple rote memorization and manipulation of formulas.

The more determinedly "un" unschooling families favor an approach to math that emphasizes conceptual understanding over simple rote memorization and manipulation of formulas. We make that choice on the assumption that our children will learn basic math facts and computation skills through their everyday activities. This often means that they learn those basic arithmetic operations at later ages than traditionally occurs in schools, but it also means that when they do, they learn more quickly and easily. Because they not only see the real-world applications, but participate in them directly, math skills are not abstract and arbitrary lessons but real, working tools.

Toddlers and preschoolers start playing around with the idea of number (this many is "three"; this is "threeness") quite early, before we really think of them as doing math:

We do counting games. Grouping and sorting appears to have developed pretty naturally, as they sort colored Duplo and some small rubber toys that are sortable by color or kind (i.e., all the cars, or all the orange cars, trucks, and boats . . .). Arithmetic is "current" for us; we're simply showing our eldest how it works, using fingers or objects to add, and it's a game. We'll simply ask him out of the blue what 2 + 2 is. Meanwhile, some six months ago, at the dinner table, he suddenly explained to his brother that if you had four french fries and ate one, you'd have three. Voilà, subtraction. —*Patrick*, California

So far it has just been a natural progression. We begin counting and sorting with preschoolers, as soon as they seem to get the idea. We might count or sort toys, or anything else we're working with. We played with patterns, then, too. We encourage problem-solving by *not* jumping up and trying to solve things for the kids, or by asking questions that will help them along. Fractions begin with sharing of food, measuring for baking, and so on. We've had some basic workbooks; for instance, dot-to-dots are fun for counting practice. But doing anything in the workbooks is totally optional for the kids. —*Grace*, California

Once kids begin to grasp numbers and counting, the steps they take to begin to understand more can vary tremendously, depending on the style and interests of their family. Some kids are taken with cooking and learn to figure fractions in the course of doubling or halving recipes. Others are builders, and discover measuring, estimating, and the beginnings of geometry by constructing a doghouse or a planter box, or even by devising a new Lego castle. Still others find that money opens doors:

I still laugh at how my daughter learned most of her arithmetic. She had no interest at all until we started giving her a fairly substantial allowance—enough for her to be the one to pay for most of the books and toys she wanted. Suddenly she was figuring out how long it would take her to save for more expensive items, and how much money she would have left at various rates of saving. Then we told her about banks and interest, and she got really hooked! (When she was spending her own money, she got much pickier about what she wanted, too.) —*Ann*, California

Based on our math experience in school, most of us tend to think of learning mathematics as a rigidly sequential, progressive process. We assume that we cannot learn any "higher" mathematics—whatever that may be— until we have mastered all of the "basics." Most of us get

so bogged down in those basics somewhere in junior high or high school that we never get beyond the purely computational.

But mathematics is so much more: pattern recognition, sorting, measurement, logic, problem-solving, probability, statistics, topology, and much more. If we let ourselves begin to look at it all, it's hard to avoid seeing math everywhere. And almost anything we do involves math in one way or another. This makes it easy for unschooled kids to become comfortable with the concepts and processes that are "math."

> If we let ourselves begin to look at it all, it's hard to avoid seeing math everywhere. And almost anything we do involves math in one way or another.

I see math as a major challenge. Without the America Online homeschoolers, particularly Christine Webb, I'd still be thinking of math as something done in a book rather than a tool used in life. And I should know better, since I graduated with a degree in electrical engineering! I'm still trying to break that mindset and see that building with blocks, sorting, and observing patterns are really math—and that memorizing the times table is not math.

The times table strikes fear into lots of folk. It seems so fundamental to math, when it's merely computation. What is important is understanding what addition is, what multiplication is, and why that period is mixed in with the numbers, and most of all, estimation. You're in deep sneakers if you rely on a memorized table and forget one or memorize one wrong. Most of the table can be picked up naturally. The holes can be filled in by understanding the concept of multiplication: that 8×7 is just the easy 8×5 plus two more 8's. It seems senseless to spend all of third grade memorizing the times table rather than twenty minutes in sixth grade. (My five-year-old daughter already knows what two sixes are. She plays with dice! So she's got part of the table memorized already.)

And how can you learn math without pages and pages of practice? It's just as effective and a lot more fun to play games (like Monopoly and blackjack) that use math than to do number problem after number problem. And there's no incentive to get the umpteenth number-problem right, as there is when drawing up plans for a birdhouse.

We do lots of counting whenever we come across it in daily life. She gets a kick out of it, so it's no burden to her. I mention fractions when I'm cutting pizza or brownies and when we're following a recipe. She loves sorting, so that comes naturally. We occasionally use the Miquon Math workbook and others, but not in any formal way. They're more like puzzles to her than workbooks. Occasionally we'll do word problems: How many legs do four cats have? If you have five cats and three leave, then six more come, how many cats do you have? We play board games in which she has to add two dice together to move her piece. We have math manipulatives (pattern blocks, tangrams, Cuisenaire rods, geoboards), but they aren't used in any formal way either. Basically, they're just toys to her. And we have Edmark's *Mighty Math, Millie's Math House,* and *Anno's Learning Games* for the computer.

We don't divorce math from real life. This is the hard part: to recognize math all around you: recipes, games, cutting a pizza, noticing patterns, games, unit pricing, money, games. And did I mention games? I've been convinced by other homeschoolers that all math through the second grade or so can be learned from life if you're open to seeing it.
—Joyce, Massachusetts

I know that math seems to be one area where unschoolers lose faith; it seems that counting must precede addition which must precede subtraction, etc., etc. It isn't so. What we have done is to explore math. We spent one July, when Dan was six and Ben two years old, poring through a picture book about lines. Checkerboards and sidewalks became our graph paper. We talked about and played with slopes and intersects. We discovered the relationships between the different kinds of lines, both physically and in their mathematical representations. The biggest number we used was four, as that was the biggest number Ben could really comprehend—and comprehension of "fourness" is different from knowing how to recite numbers up to fifty.

We have continued to mess about with mathematics. Arithmetic skills come along. Because they need and use the math—measuring and comparing volumes, weights, sizes, rates, costs, and so forth—the math they learn stays learned. Ben, however, reversed my concepts of learning math through need. He desperately wanted to play a computer game that required single-figure addition and subtraction facts. He asked for a chart with all the facts on it, and quickly memorized them so as to play the game more quickly. His chart-reading skills are exceptionally good, though.

We have math tools all around us: balances, measuring tapes of many kinds, Cuisenaire rods, timers, rules, and graph paper with large one-inch squares, as well as the standard and logarithmic varieties. We had a number-line from 20 to 100 around the dining room when the twelve numerals on a clock face were outgrown for use as a mini-number-line.

I have found that their schooled friends may indeed be quicker on straight computation, but Dan and Ben have a better sense of computation—better estimation skills. Where it might be easy to compute some number as 126 or 12.6, Dan can tell you that the one makes sense because the answer needs to be between 100 and 150.

Educational television has also played a part. *Square One* was the best, being entertaining and showing that math can be fun as well as useful. Dan and Ben also enjoyed a number of the fifteen-minute math programs [on instructional television] that usually explain a mathematical concept with some story involved. These are useful so that concepts not yet needed can become familiar without pressure. I especially liked the fact that they often showed multiple ways to reach the same result.

Dan and Ben have been free to explore mathematics. There is joy in the discovery of odd and even numbers that each had, but which I was cheated of because it was taught to me. Dan worked out probability for the sheer pleasure of it, and Ben has been messing about with exponents and their properties. And as parents, we had not only the delight of the first step, the first word read, but that first equation solved as well.
—*Cindy, Wisconsin*

Games of all kinds are a great way for kids to become comfortable with numbers. Card games—blackjack, poker, cribbage, hearts, even solitaire—involve not only addition but patterns and probability. And to play them well requires fairly quick thinking. Most board games also use at least counting and basic addition, and many—such as Monopoly and Yahtzee—require more complicated calculations and decision-making.

There are also plenty of manipulatives designed expressly for mathematical learning. Cuisenaire rods—cubes, rods, and squares based on the decimal counting system—are probably the best known of these, although building toys such as Lego and K'nex offer similar insights. Pattern blocks—flat blocks in several shapes such as diamonds, squares, triangles, and so on—are also popular and develop skills in geometric design and pattern recognition.

Many families find that half the fun comes with do-it-yourself manipulatives. Craft sticks (you can buy them cheaply in bulk at craft stores, or just eat *lots* of popsicles and save the sticks) can be used for counting, for making geometric designs, for building, and for any number of other projects, as can toothpicks, marbles, clay beads, loose change, and even edibles like jelly beans or M&Ms.

The big advantage to such a laid-back approach to math is that you can back off on pushing those basic skills and let your kids get comfortable and familiar with all the quietly math-related material all around them. Especially with kids who've had bad experiences with math in school, it usually pays to let them come to math on their own instead of dragging them, kicking and screaming all the way.

> Especially with kids who've had bad experiences with math in school, it usually pays to let them come to math on their own instead of dragging them, kicking and screaming all the way.

When we started homeschooling, I used Miquon Math, which uses Cuisenaire rods, plus a lot of other manipulative stuff (geoboard, pattern blocks, googolplex). I think it provided a very good number sense—and for a while she liked it. What has been the most successful has been just making up problems as we go along, using whatever interest she has at the moment. Most concepts come easily, but she gets frustrated if she doesn't understand something quickly, so I have to be very careful not to push. We have done very little formal math this year, but she frequently talks about things mathematical and incorporates math into her activities. Her learning style has always been to wait until something is easy and then just make a leap. This goes in spades for math. She has no interest in working at it, but seems to have no trouble just absorbing it at her own pace. It gets easier and easier to find ways to work it into everyday life. She plays a few math CD-ROM games, and especially enjoys the ones that stress logic and creative thinking. —*Stefani,* New Hampshire

We play math games. The kids like Yahtzee and dominoes (the rule is you have to add your own score), and they love Monopoly Junior. They also like Connect Four (prediction/strategy) and Chutes and Ladders (counting to 100), and they are always playing with Lego. There are a lot of other games that they play that are made up, like the grocery store scenario, for instance, that involve math skills. Throughout all of our unschooling efforts, though, both kids have thrived on timed math tests. We have a computer program that I downloaded from the Internet that prints out a sheet of thirty math problems (all four arithmetic operations), and they ask me to give them three to five minutes (depending on skill) to complete them. It's a great way to build their speed, skill, and memory—but if I were them, I wouldn't have asked for it! Kids—go figure! —*Laura Y.,* California

I think we did most of the early arithmetic just through living. My son had trouble with early math facts like addition and subtraction, so we played daily games of "adding" or "subtracting" Uno, where you had to do the appropriate operation with the card below before you could play your card. We have half a shelf full of arithmetic and math books, which rarely if ever get used and never consistently. We also have Cuisenaire rods, which we used in the early school years, and the game Set, which we still sometimes play. To date, my daughter has largely avoided higher math. If and when she wants it, we'll do it in whatever way it takes (Clonlara's Compuhigh, community college, textbook, whatever). —*Carol,* Florida

Math, argh! Math and I were intuitively obvious to each other until I went to school. I could count and manipulate patterns and logic at a very early age. It was not until second grade when I was given timed math tests every day—one hundred addition and subtraction problems to be done in ninety seconds—that I began to hate it. No matter what I did, I could never get it right. I either took too long, or the teacher couldn't read my handwriting. It wasn't that I didn't know the answers; I did, but I always got so nervous that I couldn't think clearly. Since then, you say "math" and I want to scream and cry. I still don't like it. If you don't call it math I can do it, but call it math—or especially algebra—and forget it! I put up the block that there is no point in learning it. But the funny thing is that in the past few months, I have realized that if math is patterns and logic and relationships and music, then what is *not* math? Now I have decided that everything is math in one sense or another. So I don't worry about whether I know algebra or not; ever since I was little, I could solve algebraic problems without needing some stupid formula to do it. But I still don't know what I am going to do about the two math credits I have to earn for high school. Deal with it later! —*Chase,* Florida

My daughter has hated math since she was in school doing worksheets. We have done a few worksheets in preparation for standardized tests, but she often ended up in tears. Using Marilyn Burns' *I Hate Mathematics* book was a little more successful. She has also discovered that logic problems are actually fun and the game Yahtzee is fun. Almost any game will do. However, she gets most of her math education from shopping and cooking and other real-world problem solving. We co-led a homeschool math club this year based on the Math Olympiad. She couldn't do most of the problems, but she enjoyed the social aspects and seemed to absorb some new math concepts. Occasionally she feels anxious that she's not keeping up with her age-mates, and she'll do some textbook math or sit down with me as I explain some math process. This almost always generates stress, and we are doing it less and less. Another blind alley I have followed is bribery. Last year, I offered her a generous monetary incentive if she learned her times tables by the end of the year. She was ecstatic about the deal. But even though she loves spending money and I reminded her of the deal periodically, she never spent more than fifteen minutes on the project the whole year. Interestingly enough, I notice that more and more often, when the times tables crop up in real life, she knows the answers somehow. I feel that my major task with her will be alleviating her math anxiety.

My son, on the other hand, enjoys math. He used to ask to do Miquon Math worksheets and sailed through several of the books. His computational skills are weak from lack of practice, but he has a solid understanding of concepts. I feel confident that, with his interest, he will eventually polish his computational skills. —*Carolyn*, Pennsylvania

Math has never been high in the interests of anyone in our household. They all have been mildly interested in basic math concepts as young children, and quite capable of learning them. We have done math concepts in a very casual way, as the girls would ask for it. I'm afraid that, beyond that level, neither my husband nor I are very helpful! Amie, at about the age of twelve, decided that she didn't want to do math at all anymore, and rather than fight about it, I decided that if she really needed math for pursuing an interest or higher education, she'd get it when she needed it. This is precisely what happened. Her interests were in fine art and music, and to get into art college she only needed to have a GED. She spent a couple of weeks casually studying the GED book, and did some of the math pretests in it. She had a friend who was doing well in high school come over to help her a couple of times. I remember the friend turning to me with exasperation and telling me, "She doesn't do the problems right, but she comes up with the right answers!" She'd found her own ways of computing. I was interested once to hear a mathematician who home-schooled his family say that he didn't believe in teaching them math—that the way mathematics is taught is too narrow, and he wanted his children to see more possibilities.

When Anika started school at the age of twelve, they gave her a placement test. She tested ahead of her age in language arts, but at grade three in math. The fact that she'd never taken a test before probably had a bit to do with it, but she had refused to have anything to do with math for several years. They decided to have her do her math with the learning-assistance teacher. This overworked teacher said, "Your mother is used to teaching you at home; here is the workbook, do half an hour in it every night." Anika was in Late French Immersion and the homework was staggering. She sat and worked for three hours every day after a full day of school. I simply couldn't make her do an additional half-hour of math after that. We forgot the workbook. One Friday in December, Anika came home and said, "The learning teacher wants to see my math workbook on Monday." Panic! She finished the book in two long sittings that weekend. On Monday they tested her again, and she tested grade six in math.

—*Terry*, British Columbia

Q: What are your favorite things to do?

S H A U N A (1 3) : My favorite things are reading and dancing. Dancing isn't really sit-down formal learning, but I'm learning just the same. Math is something I really want to be good at, but it has not always been easy. I'm thirteen. If I were in school, I'd be in eighth grade, doing pre-algebra or, at most, beginning algebra. I've finished trigonometry and am going to start pre-calculus soon. Trigonometry was hard at many times, and algebra was quite frustrating. But I needed to understand to move on to the next level. If I ran into something I didn't understand, the algebra book would go flying! Then I'd go rescue it, and ask my dad to translate it into English so I could understand it.

Terry's daughter's experience is fairly common. Time after time, unschoolers who have done no formal math for years find that it takes very little effort to catch up with their formally instructed peers. And without the enforced drudgery of worksheets that is still all too common in modern mathematics instruction, they avoid developing an attitude that math is something hard and abstract that only other "smarter" people do, and become comfortable and competent users of their math skills.

But what about all that "higher" math? How do unschoolers learn all those arcane mathematical topics their parents are too intimidated themselves to tackle? What do you do when your child's mathematical knowledge exceeds your own and she still wants more?

What you do is help her find what she needs in order to learn what she's interested in. This may mean trolling through bookstores and libraries to find the right books, or getting a new programming language for a computer, or even enrolling in a correspondence or community college math course. If your child isn't quite sure where she wants to go next, you may want to look for someone knowledgeable about math to advise her. This could be as easy as consulting friends or one of the Internet resources (the Home Ed list's "math cabal" and AOL's homeschooling math mavens offer great ideas and advice), or you might want to call a local college math department for advice or to advertise for a student willing to serve as a tutor.

Jenny is now finishing up *Saxon's Advanced Math* (pre-calculus) and has purchased another pre-calculus book from the community college book store. She wants to take calculus next fall at the community college, where they are using a book that is heavily into using a graphing calculator, which isn't Saxon's approach at all. She has been beyond me in math for a while, but using logic I could usually answer her questions. A couple of months ago, I found her a tutor who sees her for an hour every week or three to answer her questions, and this saves me a lot of time.
—*Joanne, Virginia*

The important thing to remember about the child who is entranced and consumed by mathematics is that you will not need to keep up with her yourself. With only a little help, she will find her own way. She'll make up her own problems and puzzles, just to see if she can solve them, and keep looking for new problems she hasn't yet tackled. She'll look for the kinds of learning materials and helpers she wants, and will let you know what help she needs from you. She is the one doing the learning, and you wouldn't be able to stop her if you tried.

Resources

Anno, Mitsumasa. *Anno's Math Games* (Paper Star, 1997).

Anno, Mitsumasa. *Anno's Math Games II* (Paper Star, 1997).

Anno, Mitsumasa. *Anno's Math Games III* (Paper Star, 1997). Aimed at ages four through eight, Anno's appealing books introduce a few fundamental math tools (such as Cartesian coordinate systems) with the illustrator's usual style and flair.

Burns, Marilyn. *The Book of Think: Or, How to Solve a Problem Twice Your Size* (Little, Brown & Co., 1976).

Burns, Marilyn. *The I Hate Mathematics! Book* (Little, Brown & Co., 1976).

Burns, Marilyn. *Math for Smarty Pants* (Little, Brown & Co., 1982). Part of the Brown Paper School Book series, these Burns titles are a great introduction to everyday math and problem-solving.

Cuisenaire Company of America, P.O. Box 5026, White Plains, NY 10602-5026; 800-237-3142. Cuisenaire offers a variety of books and math manipulatives in addition to Cuisenaire rods.

Huff, Darrell. *How to Lie with Statistics* (W.W. Norton & Co., 1993). This classic, originally published in 1954, is still one of the best books ever on how charts and statistics are used to mislead—and how to detect such misuse.

Jacobs, Harold. *Mathematics: A Human Endeavor: A Book for Those Who Think They Don't Like the Subject* (W.H. Freeman & Co., 1994). Jacobs' text is actually fun, with lots of open-ended activities. It introduces ideas on counting and permutations, mathematical curves and solids, probability, topology, and statistics. Aimed at high-school-age students, but accessible to the interested younger learner as well. Jacobs has also written algebra and geometry texts.

Key Curriculum Press, P.O. Box 2304, Berkeley, CA 94702; 800-995-MATH. Key publishes Miquon Math workbooks and manipulatives for younger learners, and the "Key To" series for older students. Available in the "Key To" series are sets on fractions, decimals, measurement, algebra, and geometry.

Pappas, Theoni. *The Joy of Mathematics* (Wide World Publishing, 1989).

Pappas, Theoni. *More Joy of Mathematics: Exploring Mathematics All Around You* (Wide World Publishing, 1991). These collections of short, three- to four-page presentations on all kinds of "real world" math are perfect for unschoolers.

Polya, George. *How to Solve It: A New Aspect of Mathematical Method* (Princeton University Press, 1988). This is another classic, originally published in 1945. Polya uses geometric examples to illustrate methods and rules applicable to solving any kind of problem.

Saxon Math, Saxon Publishers, Inc., 1300 McGee, Suite 100, Norman, OK 73072. Saxon Math seems to be either loved or hated; it is very skills-oriented and heavy on the exercise sets; probably not for those who like to speculate about mathematical ideas.

Stanmark, Jean Kerr, Virginia Thompson, and Ruth Cossey. *Family Math* (Equals, 1986). *Family Math* is a popular collection of math activities from the Lawrence Hall of Science. Some activities are too workbook-like, but there is lots of good material nonetheless.

Internet Resources

Natural Math (www.naturalmath.com). Maria Droujkova and Dmitri Droujkov have created in this Web site an outstanding collection of activities and resources for learning and doing math. Their material is designed especially for an unschooling approach, and is usable by almost anyone of any age who is interested in exploring mathematics.

CHAPTER SEVEN

Science

SCIENCE IS MUCH like math and most of the other topics we peek at in these chapters. Unschoolers are mystified with the science version of that question we hear so often: How do children learn science? How, we wonder, could they *not* learn science?

Again, as with math, the mystery is partly due to differences in what we mean by learning "science"—whether we mean a sort of scientific literacy that each individual should possess, or explicit preparation for a professional life in science. Most unschoolers, in science as in any other field, simply believe that a child's passion for a particular field will become apparent in the course of achieving that basic literacy—and that, once ignited, it will lead that child far more effectively than the most rigorously taught laboratory science course.

Getting started on basic scientific literacy is easy. Science is largely a matter of attitude, a way of looking at the world to learn as much as we can about it. This scientific outlook consists of several steps:

1.   Observation: looking carefully at the subject of study, noticing as much as we can about it.

2.   Prediction: using our observations as the basis of predicting future behavior, either of our specific subject or of other similar subjects.

> Science is largely a matter of attitude, a way of looking at the world to learn as much as we can about it.

3.   Experimentation (or "trial and error"): testing the prediction against reality, and revising predictions based on the new observations acquired.

Children, from earliest infancy, are natural scientists. They spend most of their waking hours observing, predicting, and testing those predictions in a constant effort to understand their world. From smiling and vocalizing and noticing that some people return such gestures, to tossing food to the floor and discovering that it doesn't usually come back, babies progress through scores of difficult concepts such as gravity, locomotion, and language. As unschooling parents of younger children, all we need to do is keep our kids supplied with fodder for their observation and experimentation (and keep them and ourselves safe in the process!).

Right now, at ages seven and ten, we learn science by exploring. First, we try to create a rich learning environment. We have several shelves of books about science. We have posters under clear plastic on the kitchen table. We have toys—things like pulleys and gears, magnifying glasses, and binoculars—lying around. We use computer software. We often do "quickie" trips to the local nature center, the zoo, the science museum, and the natural history museum. We find that it's very important when we visit these places to allow the children to specialize—to take our time on only one or two exhibits and to keep it short. For example, we may spend an hour looking at the dinosaur bones and fifteen minutes in the rocks and minerals, and skip the rest of the museum. Having a membership in the institutions takes the economic pressure off these visits.

After setting up an environment for the kids, we watch for some interest to grow. When Comet Hale-Bopp was out there, we learned about comets by reading, spending several evenings observing, and taking in a special planetarium show on comets. Seeing the movie *Volcano* has sparked an interest in lava and magma and, hence, rocks. We've purchased a field guide to rocks, and we intend to do some collecting now, and testing in the field. When someone we know has an illness or injury, we learn more about the body. The children also take some outside classes—some with the homeschool support group, and some day camps sponsored by the zoo and museum. Both of them are still science generalists; neither has become particularly knowledgeable about any one field.
—*Carolyn*, Pennsylvania

Science is like math and other stuff; it happens when something sparks. I view science as having two parts: there's the "facts and trivia" part about knowing that plants need sunlight and water is H_2O, and there's the part about setting up an experiment to find out something. We try to do both. Andy has learned an incredible amount from videos. He watches *Nova*, *Discovery 2000*, *Newton's Apple*, and all sorts of other stuff. He isn't as much into doing things as he is into organizing things and understanding them, though he does lots with Lego Technic—engineering stuff that loses me.

Sarah is the doer. We plant things and watch them grow, then change things and see what happens. She mixes things and lets them dry out. I want to start writing things down and predicting outcomes with her this summer if she's ready for that step. She isn't as much into absorbing trivia as Andy is. Sarah likes to tie things to her own experiences. —*Ruth*, Montana

Most unschooled kids seem to enthusiastically pursue what used to be called "natural history." Many explore nature, looking at both plants and animals and how they grow, at rocks and minerals and habitats, at the sky both day and night, at everything they see in front of them. Others are more interested in understanding how things work; more than a few unschooling parents become avid collectors of used or broken small appliances and other gadgets for their mechanically minded offspring. For many, television provides a trigger for further exploration:

We infrequently pull a chapter from one of the science textbooks we've culled from the depository, but most of our science is either Discovery Channel, Learning Channel, or PBS. There is a wealth of information there, especially for this young age. Rory loves experiments and has been mesmerized with the vinegar-and-baking-soda volcano for weeks now, so some easy experiment books are around where they'll fall into his hands. When he received a balsa-wood glider plane, it was easy to have the books on the physics of flight lying about. Hallie loves to cook, and we've talked about the different properties of ingredients she uses, and what grew from the ground, etc. She's gotten a new cookbook for her collection which more directly involves science in the kitchen. —*Jo, Lousiana*

So far we've done a lot of fooling around with various sciences. There are lots of TV shows that have sparked her interest, and lots and lots of books about specific subjects (origins of life, cells, space, wildlife, etc.). We've done a little chemistry from a set, and have been to the Science Museum of Boston several times. We use our surroundings for natural science and talk about everything when we're outside walking in the woods. She has been busy this spring making nature notebooks, observing birds, frogs, and salamanders. This week she's been watching a *Connections* festival on the Learning Channel, which has her totally in its grip—such an incredible blend of science and history. —*Stefani, New Hampshire*

We went through a stretch when the girls were little—maybe four and seven—when they'd collect rocks, leaves, twigs, and other small items on every walk we took. My pockets used to be loaded by the time we got back. What was interesting was to see what different things they did with what they collected. Elisabeth would draw what she found, being as precise as she could about colors and shapes, which would sometimes show up in other drawings she did later. Lynne would sort and resort her finds, into all kinds of different categories. But they both ended up telling me a lot about the things they found. —*Ann, California*

In many unschooling families with younger children, science is a family activity—a matter of shared excursions and projects. The particular area of science they explore doesn't much matter. In fact, they may focus on a broad topic—rain forests, say—that involves several distinct scientific fields: botany, zoology, ecology, biochemistry, meteorology, and so on. What's important is again that prime requisite for unschooling in any subject: curiosity. When parents show their own curiosity about what they see—whatever it may be—and explore further to learn more, they send a far stronger message about what science is and how it works than the most colorful and appealing textbook ever could. If you are interested in science in general, or in some specific field, and your interest is obvious and enthusiastic, your kids will tend to indulge their curiosity as well—even though their own interests may turn out to be in other fields altogether.

Q: How do you find out about things you want to do or learn about?

RORY (8): I just feel like doing them. I ask my parents, sometimes go on the Internet but not much. Sometimes when I want to do a math problem or something, I just look in my math book.

HALLIE (6): Usually I ask my parents, and I never go on the Internet because my mother's usually on it when I ask her the question!

The basic tools for indulging scientific curiosity are neither complicated nor esoteric and, with one or two exceptions, are quite inexpensive:

- paper and writing utensils: a notebook or sketchbook in which to record observations is the most basic tool

- magnifying glass: a good magnifying glass focuses attention on a small area, not only allowing you to see more detail but encouraging you to look for detail

- microscope: when the small objects become too small for the magnifying glass, a sturdy microscope such as Brock Optical's Magiscope (which has few moving parts and requires no illuminator; see Resources at the end of this chapter) can be used satisfactorily both at home and in the field, and is relatively inexpensive

- binoculars: a decent pair is always useful, especially for astronomy; you get a wider field of view than from most inexpensive small telescopes, with nearly as much magnification

- telescope: when the binoculars are no longer enough, you can get both better magnification and a wide field of view with a six- or eight-inch Dobsonian-mount reflecting telescope, for about same price as a much smaller refracting telescope

Beyond these basics, the tools and materials your family needs for science will depend entirely on your own tastes and interests. While they'll show similarities, no two families (or even two kids) will follow the same course, as these half-dozen demonstrate:

Science is an area that comes extremely easily for Allyson. Living where we do now, she has the whole outdoors as her lab. We have a huge garden and are planning goats and chickens soon. We used to camp in a great area in California, where a local astronomy club would come to view the stars at night. They would always explain what they were doing and let the campers look through the telescopes. It was a great experience, and has sparked an interest in astronomy for all of us. We're planning to purchase a telescope and also a microscope soon. —*Terri,* Colorado

Since my husband is a scientist, science has always surrounded them in conversations, demonstrations, and lectures from Dad. We generally explored whatever they were interested in at the time. We've used *Science Experiments You Can Eat,* by Vicki Cobb, and whatever else comes from the library to answer the current interest. We have found books by Isaac Asimov to be wonderful resources. Chase has done most of her physics through his three-volume set on the topic. We have never used textbooks for science. Gardening, caring for pets, cooking, and health issues further round out our science. —*Carol,* Florida

When Dan and Ben were four and eight, they had a consuming interest in the sea. Dan loved the technology that people used to explore it; Ben preferred the life found there. We tied these together by building a coral reef in the basement with friends. There were many art projects involved in creating the reef, its creatures, sounds, and light. We designed our own "scuba gear." What I learned, though, was the power of hands-on work. I had "known" for years that water pressure increases with depth, and that a snorkel longer than fourteen inches was too long to change the air in the tube because of that pressure—but making a twenty-four-inch tube and trying to blow bubbles through it was a simple but really impressive demonstration of that pressure. It took blowing as hard as I could to get any bubbles at all.

Science is not a matter of true facts and right answers; it is an approach to knowledge that always leaves a tincture of doubt. Observation—close and thoughtful observation—followed by reflection, questioning, and more observation are what make science what it is—and unschoolers have the luxury to be able to do these things well. If we take the time to understand something thoroughly, the adjoining ideas come more easily—but taking this time is something that classroom science rarely affords. To state what you want to know as a question, figure out how to answer that question, and then make the observations and tests necessary is what both professional scientists and unschoolers can do. —*Cindy*, Wisconsin

I have to admit that most of the activities at our house are science related, and that all other subjects are learned while exploring the sciences. My children love the sciences. I find this wonderful, and encourage it. We use a tremendous number of resource materials (mostly books out of the library), and find that the best manipulatives are a good pair of binoculars and a magnifying glass.

Last year we raised praying mantises (and plan to again this year). The entire family learned a huge amount. It is amazing how much you can learn about such an interesting creature just by inviting it into your home.

Each person in our family has their own specialty in science. My husband and oldest son share a love of astronomy, and my son extends this to a passion for the planets and their moons. My younger son's passion seems to be mechanics. I love biology in its many forms. Each of us seems to get dragged into the others' interests, just because we do so many things together. Seeing the wonder and excitement through the eyes of a child is a wonderful way of becoming exposed to something new. —*Kathy*, Illinois

To be totally honest, I worried about science and unschooling when we first started, but we have done more scientific studies since we started unschooling. We have planted every seed we could find, and have learned about all their parts, and what they need to grow and live. We have learned about harvesting, and why farmers are important to our society. All of that stemmed from one packet of seeds we bought at the grocery store. Now our home is a veritable jungle!

We started collecting caterpillars (as a natural kid thing), and have now hatched several butterflies and moths in our home. It's always an exciting process—watching the chrysalis form and waiting not-so-patiently for the new bug to emerge. The kids made a poster (all on their own) of this life cycle, and have it hanging over the butterfly-hatching canopy that we bought. They like to go back and look at it every so often. They also have hatched tadpoles into frogs, and are waiting now to receive some salamander tadpoles. The caterpillar thing led naturally into insects. They started collecting them, watching their habits, and creating habitats for them indoors (within a bug cage, of course!). They also began trying to identify the different kinds of bugs they found. Through this they discovered words like "arachnid" and "myriapod," and love showing off their new vocabulary and knowledge of what characterizes all these different categories. They began exploring the bugs further by using microscopes (a Christmas gift) and magnifying glasses, and finally (to my chagrin) began dissecting these little creatures "to see what we can see," and then began labeling all their parts.

They watched a program on bats and began taking an interest in caves. This led to learning about the different layers of the earth, right down to the core. Of course, this led to a big-time interest in volcanoes and such, and they even built their own volcano and erupted it with the vinegar/baking soda mixture.

Of course, when Hale-Bopp was in the news, the children became mini-astronomers for a time. Actually, this has really stuck with them. They became interested in what made up a comet and how it traveled around the sun, and built a tiny model of a comet. They then naturally became interested in the solar system and built a papier-mâché model of it as well. There was a lunar eclipse soon after the comet became the highlight of our lives, and that sealed it! They began exploring what caused the different moon phases and what causes eclipses. Our house nearly became an observatory of sorts. And I was worried that my five- and seven-year-olds wouldn't learn enough about science! —*Laura Y.,* California

I tested out of science and math when I entered college, so I haven't had either for almost twenty-five years. That probably contributes to my insecurity in these areas. Science, for us, is discovery about the world. Nature is no problem. We have raised lots of different critters; we walk and observe, find and classify, and have tons of books for reference. I always buy educational toys and games: ant farms, aquaria, magnets, batteries, microscopes and slides, binoculars and telescopes, and lots of books. Jordan has a nature collection: fossils, bones, owl pellets, rocks, feathers, etc. Caleb likes physical science: batteries, machines, solar collectors, stuff like that. They both consider themselves to be knowledgeable about science. So do I. When they express the desire to know about something, Dan and I do our best to supply them with the resources and materials they need.

By the way, I don't arrange any experiments or activities for science. That seems disjointed and artificial to me. The kids do their own impromptu experiments when they want to know something. They try to figure things out for themselves, not reenact what someone else figured out years ago. (I have, however, read them biographies of famous scientists, but more as history than science.) —*Susan, Iowa*

Books, of course, are valuable tools for learning about science—especially specialized topics that might be too difficult, expensive, or dangerous to tackle hands-on. Often a well-written children's book on a specialized field can be the perfect introduction for either child or adult since it's designed to be especially clear and jargon-free. Such books usually include at least a limited bibliography for those interested in pursuing the subject.

Also useful are those scientific biographies and memoirs Susan mentions. Seeing what a particular discovery was like from the point of view of the discoverer can be fascinating, and comparing the perspectives of a variety of participants—as is possible with accounts of the building of the first atomic bomb, for instance—can be particularly instructive. For kids considering a field as a profession, such books can provide a glimpse at a possible way of life.

Even for kids (and their parents) who are not interested in scientific careers, books about scientific undertakings and discoveries can put those events into historical context. They can tell us about the changes that scientific discoveries have wrought, and help us to consider the effects of current and developing technologies.

While elementary science textbooks are generally as simplistic and disappointing as any textbooks—try to find a clear, straightforward, and accurate discussion of evolution, for instance—there are a few good texts at the secondary level. But for good, up-to-date material in many fields, you're probably better off looking for good "popular" science books at your local bookstore. Donald Johanson and Richard Leakey in anthropology, Robert Bakker and Stephen Jay Gould in paleontology, Freeman Dyson and the late Richard Feynman in physics, among countless others, have written engagingly and clearly of their own work and that of others in their fields. Since the publishing cycle for trade books is much less lengthy and involved than that for textbooks, the books you find in bookstores are far more likely to be current. (And any biases they show will be far more explicit than those of more "authoritative" textbooks.)

Sometimes, of course, a textbook may be just what your child wants. A teen who plans to study medicine or engineering, or who seeks admission to a college with a strict "lab science" requirement, may decide she wants a fairly conventional course of study. Helping her to find a good textbook and letting her work on her own may be all the help she needs, or she may opt for a more structured course by correspondence or at a local community college.

Whether your older student chooses to work mainly on her own or through a formal course of some kind, it may be helpful to find a mentor. As in other subject areas, this could be simply a friend or acquaintance with some expertise, a college student willing to work with her off and on, or a professor or working professional in the field. The exact nature of any mentor/learner relationship—advice, tutoring, part-time work—should be worked out by the participants.

Resources

Even more than the other chapter resource lists in this book, this list is only an idiosyncratic sampling of the types of science material unschoolers use. Think of it not as a definitive guide, but as merely suggestions for directions you can take.

Books

Amdahl, Kenn. *There Are No Electrons: Electronics for Earthlings* (Clearwater Publishing, 1991). Amdahl's approach to explaining is unusual, to say the least. It's funny, it reads like a novel, and it's actually clear and understandable.

Anderson, Alan, Gwen Diehn, and Terry Krautwurst. *Geology Crafts for Kids: 50 Nifty Projects to Explore the Marvels of Planet Earth* (Sterling Publications, 1996). This book, written for ages nine through twelve, contains not just the nifty activities but plenty of information about and illustrations of the geology they are meant to demonstrate.

Bakker, Robert T. *The Dinosaur Heresies: New Theories Unlocking the Mystery of the Dinosaurs and Their Extinction* (Kensington Publishing Corp., 1996). What we know about dinosaurs changes almost daily, it seems, and Bakker is right in the midst of the debates over the newest findings. He provides a good look into scientific investigation and controversy, as well as at the latest dinosaur findings.

Cassidy, John. *The Aerobie Book: An Inquiry into the World's Ultimate Flying Mini-Machine* (Klutz Press, 1989).

Cassidy, John. *The Explorabook: A Kid's Science Museum in a Book* (Klutz Press, 1992).

Cassidy, John. *Zap Science: A Scientific Playground in a Book* (Klutz Press, 1997). Klutz Press publishes some of the best kids' books around about science. Just ask any of the parents who keep borrowing them from their children!

Cobb, Vicki. *Science Experiments You Can Eat* (HarperTrophy, 1994). Cobb's book provides instructions and explanations for just what the title says: edible lab projects!

Cornell, Joseph Bharat. *Sharing Nature with Children* (Crystal Clarity Publishing, 1982). This classic on outdoor activities and games has long been recommended and used by the Boy Scouts, Girl Scouts, and Audubon Society.

Dyson, Freeman. *Disturbing the Universe* (Basic Books, 1981). Dyson, a mathematical physicist who worked with Feynman, is also a wonderful writer—in this case, about his scientific work and his life in general.

Epstein, Lewis Carroll. *Thinking Physics: Practical Lessons in Critical Thinking* (Insight Press, 1995). This book is a classic favorite of good physics teachers; lots of questions to think about and lead you to more questions. For age twelve and up.

Feynman, Richard P., and Ralph Leighton. *"Surely You're Joking, Mr. Feynman": Adventures of a Curious Character* (W.W. Norton & Co., 1997).

Feynman, Richard P., and Ralph Leighton. *"What Do You Care What Other People Think?": Further Adventures of a Curious Character* (W.W. Norton & Co., 1992). These autobiographical volumes, based on the stories the Nobel-winning physicist allowed his friend Leighton to tape, are possibly the ultimate unschooling books. Feynman was indeed a curious—that is, unusual—character. But even more, he was curious—insatiable in seeking out answers to questions that challenged him, whether they concerned quantum electrodynamics, the cause of the Challenger explosion, or whether he could find solely by smell which book in the bookcase his wife had most recently held. For Feynman, *finding out* was most of the fun in life, and he never stopped learning.

Gonick, Larry, and Mark Wheelis. *The Cartoon Guide to Genetics* (Harper Perennial Library, 1991).

Gonick, Larry, and Art Huffman. *The Cartoon Guide to Physics* (Harper Perennial Library, 1992). Gonick's books are good, humorous introductions to their topics.

Gould, Stephen Jay. *Dinosaur in a Haystack: Reflections in Natural History* (Crown Publishers, 1996). Gould, an evolutionary paleontologist who specializes in marine snails, is also a gifted and eloquent writer. This title is the seventh volume of collections of his monthly column in *Natural History*. If you can't find this one, go for any of the others; they're all wonderful.

Hellemans, Alexander, and Brian Bunch. *The Timetables of Science: A Chronology of the Most Important People and Events in the History of Science* (Touchstone Books, 1991). This one's great for putting everything into context.

Hewitt, Paul G. *Conceptual Physics* (Addison-Wesley Publishing, 1997). This is a college-level textbook (now in its eighth edition) that teaches the concepts of physics without mathematics. It's great for those who want to know how things work instead of just plugging numbers into formulas they don't quite understand.

Medawar, Peter B. *Advice to a Young Scientist* (Basic Books, 1981). Medawar is another Nobel-winning scientist who writes well. His book is yet another good look into how science works.

Walker, Jearl, and Jean Walker. *The Flying Circus of Physics* (John Wiley & Sons, 1977). Walker looks engagingly at the physics of everyday life.

Tools

Brock Optical, Inc., 220 Live Oak Boulevard, Casselberry, FL 32707; 800-780-9111 or 407-260-9111. Brock's "Magiscope" is an amazingly tough microscope. With its few moving parts, and needing only natural light, it's easy to use and reliable.

Edmund Scientific Company, Consumer Science Division, 101 East Gloucester Pike, Barrington, NJ 08007-1380; 609-547-8880. Edmund's "Scientifics" catalog is as much fun as it's always been, with games, toys, and serious scientific tools for just about any field of science.

Society for Amateur Scientists, 4735 Claremont Square, Suite 179, San Diego, CA 92117; 800-873-8767; web2.thesphere.com/SAS/. The SAS offers lots of resources for "anyone who wants to do science simply for the love of it."

TOPS Learning Systems, 10970 S. Mulino Road, Canby, OR 97013. TOPS publishes booklets of inventive open-ended science activities using everyday objects. The unit on balancing, for example, explains how to make an equal-arm balance from a sheet of paper and folded index cards (paper clips are used as weights), and suggests plenty of ideas for trying it out.

Fun Physics (Mac only) and *Interactive Physics 2.5* (Mac/Win) are interactive physics simulation programs that allow the user to play with ropes, springs, meters, and masses, with variable constraints such as gravity and friction. Using simulations, you can model experiments that are impossible to perform in real life. Manufactured by Knowledge Revolution, they are available through the Drinking Gourd Book Company (see Resources, Chapter 2).

An Unschooling Week Two

Jo (Louisiana) says that her records are extremely informal; she keeps them in pencil in teachers' planning books, recording what the children have been doing, what they're interested in, what changes she sees in their lives, and so on. Under the Louisiana private school statute, she is not required to keep these logs, but must affirm 180 days attendance and a sustained curriculum at least equivalent to that of the public schools. But, says Jo, "Hallie likes to work from books and workbooks on a regular basis, and Rory does from time to time, so should it be necessary to indicate 'sustained curriculum,' I believe that would be easily accomplished by pulling out the books and workbooks they've gone through, which I do try to keep current in the journal."

The following week's activities from Jo's journal occurred when Hallie was six and Rory was seven.

SUNDAY:

- Watched *Keeping the Promise*, a historical drama about settling upper Maine; discussed Indians, illness, travel limitations.

MONDAY:

- Both had P.E. and basketball practice at YMCA; Hallie had dance lessons.

(continues)

TUESDAY:

- Rory read the Pee Wee Scouts book. Hallie came across me doing an Internet search and wanted to try a test. We found one at Edutest; she scored seventy-seven percent on the second-grade test. Rory and I discussed how algebraic equations are used to find an unknown.

- Hallie had a Daisy Scouts meeting; Rory and I observed. There was a relevant discussion about children's groups in church following. Rory attended his Boy Scout Pack meeting.

- Worked in atrium (a Montessori-based religious education program for children, of which I'm a catechist) for one and a half hours while I prepared materials, mostly on art works and in meditation.

WEDNESDAY:

- In conjunction with Scout awards, Rory prepared a paper and we had a discussion on freedom and American history legends.

- At Rory's Den meeting, Diana LeBlanc made a Native American presentation including the history of Native Americans, medicines, traditions, beliefs. Hallie attended, and good discussion afterward.

THURSDAY:

- Started alternate reading (Rory reads some, then Hallie, then Mom) of *The Pink Motel,* by Carol Ryrie Brink. This promises to be a keeper!

- Hallie worked in her Language Arts workbook—introduction to sentence requirements (noun, verb), and we discussed diagramming sentences. Rory had basketball practice at the Y, and piano lessons.

FRIDAY:

- Continued *Pink Motel*.

- Allowance distribution made; spent on penny candy—good counting, budgeting, estimating (taxes).

- Question: When temperature goes down and precipitation goes up, what happens? What makes it freeze? What makes snow? Discussion of atmosphere, temperature changes amongst clouds, etc.

- Good morning for field trip, so went to the State Capitol. Crews working in both chambers, and were only able to peek into the Senate chamber. Wandered around the halls some, rode the elevator to the Governor's floor. Most interesting: the bullet holes in the wall where Huey P. Long was assassinated.

- P.E. at the YMCA.

SATURDAY:

- Rory had a basketball game. He's getting somewhat discouraged with the lack of enthusiasm of the other players, and their increasing unwillingness to listen to the coach.

CHAPTER EIGHT

History

I F THERE WERE no other reason to unschool, history alone would be enough. History—along with the rest of the social sciences—is all about people: about how they lived, what and why they behaved as they did, how they made our world what it is. As unschoolers, we are not tied to the traditional text-based, chronological presentation commonly used in schools. We can de-emphasize the dates and battles and treaties in favor of trying to understand the people who made choices and struggled to make lives for themselves in decades and centuries past. We can replace that neutral-sounding passive narration ("a shorter work week of forty hours was instituted") with a whole collection of voices—workers, manufacturers, union organizers, government officials, and so on—of people who lived through events and sought to institute their own views of how society should work. And we can begin to comprehend that understanding history is not so much about memorizing hard facts as it is about realizing that there are scores of different—often contradictory—ways to interpret those facts.

Most unschooling families find that history is seldom a subject they have to work hard to cover once they let go of conventional history textbooks:

> Texts? I can't think of one that's really worth warm spit. Lots of *books* about history, but texts? Awful. Texts are to history what library paste is to a gourmet meal. —*Patrick*, California

Patrick's attitude is common among unschoolers. Why settle for learning history from textbooks when there is so much *real* history available all around us?

The first step is letting go of the idea that history must be learned strictly in chronological order, from the dawn of time right on up to the present. We're so used to thinking of history as a series of events happening in strict chronological order that it's a major shift to realize that there's no particular necessity for learning things exactly in the order in which they happened. Most kids tend to get hooked by one historical era or another; once they start digging into their period of choice, they begin to create their own context for placing other periods.

> We're so used to thinking of history as a series of events happening in strict chronological order that it's a major shift to realize that there's no particular necessity for learning things exactly in the order in which they happened.

Like many other unschooling families, my girls liked reading the books in Laura Ingalls Wilder's "Little House" series. For all the weeks we were reading them out loud in the evenings, when they heard about other historical periods they would always ask, "Was that before or after Mary and Laura?" Then, when we went to a Renaissance Faire, and later a Dickens Christmas Fair, they started looking for information and stories about those periods, and they had more eras to plug people and events into. Elisabeth got her sense of the chronology at least partly through the clothes of different eras. She found books on the history of costume, and drew dozens of sheets full of designs she found and imitated, from the early medieval period through the nineteenth century. —*Ann,* California

My goal is that the kids have an idea of the flow of time, not spend their time memorizing dates. When George Washington is brought up, I want them to get a picture of him and his world: horse travel, no phones, no TV, no castles or armor, first president, etc. We have a timeline that we occasionally mark things on, but at the moment we aren't too focused on chronology except in a very broad sense.

One thing I try to do on a daily basis is to locate some event or person in both time and space. It's as casual as asking about when and where is *Star Trek* (in the future and in outer space), to getting out the atlas and locating London, or looking up when barbed wire was invented. We even talk about what clues an author gives us in books as to the setting in time and space. —*Ruth,* Montana

There are a variety of ways to make sense of a nonchronological approach to learning history. Some families use a timeline—either a published volume or, what is perhaps even more useful, one they create themselves. Typically it's a long piece of butcher paper hung in a hallway, with centuries and perhaps decades marked; family members add information—people, events, both historical and fictional characters, inventions, ancestors, whatever catches their attention—as they come across it.

We recently had to cut down a very old oak tree. After counting the tree rings, we came back to the house and, with butcher paper, drew out a timeline. The tree sprouted around the time when Abraham Lincoln was president, so we started with that. We added dates such as our family birth-dates, Grandma's and Grandpa's birth-dates. It really seemed to tie things together. —*Cathy B.*, California

Other families find that maps are an effective means of organizing historical information. Instead of focusing on *when* events occurred, they concentrate on *where*. Some families make their own map posters, while others use printed maps from sources such as the National Geographic Society. (And, of course, other families enjoy *both* maps and timelines, while yet others get along just fine with neither.)

Whether you end up using a timeline or maps or both or neither, there are dozens of ways to explore history and how it was made. Aside from making history more interesting, they also make it easy to tie history to current events, anthropology, psychology, sociology, and all of the other "people" disciplines.

Books and Movies

The fact that history textbooks are remarkably dismal as tools for learning history does not mean that there are not good history books available. You only have to look in your local library or bookstore to discover that history is a hugely popular field. But the history books that interest most people are the books about particular events and particular people—the books that satisfy a specific inter-est. In most cases, you'll find that biographies are a good way to get a hook into a period; looking at one individual's life is a great way to start looking at a whole era.

Conversely, it's also interesting to read about lives from different periods to compare them. If you or your daughter are interested in art, for instance, you might read a biography (or several) of Michelangelo and then read more about the Renaissance, or you might concentrate on artists in general instead of on only one period, and read biographies of Michelangelo, Monet, and Picasso.

Another option not to be missed is historical fiction, whether in print or on film and video. Fiction, strangely enough, often provides a better understanding of historical events than even the most accurate factual account. The best historical fiction puts the reader in the midst of events, seeing and feeling what life was like, and brings an immediacy completely lacking in textbook accounts, however accurate they may be. With novels and movies, too, it's sometimes easier to develop a sense for inaccuracies; knowing that something is fictionalized gives you the freedom to question what you read. Once you and your kids develop the habit of questioning the truth of what you read or view, it's easy to transfer that habit to nonfiction as well.

I initially planned to "teach" history in chronological order. I'd had trouble realizing what was going on in different parts of the world at a particular time, so it seemed to make sense. Of course, that was when I was going to "teach" it all!

We read biographies or historical novels for most of our history. I'm a morning-paper addict, so our initial conversations of the day have to do with what's in the newspaper: current events, history, sociology, criminology. I have recently started becoming more serious in my genealogy hobby, and this has led to a good deal of conversation about religion, pursuit of freedom, emigration, pioneers, etc. —Jo, Louisiana

My ten-year-old daughter's history sense has been almost entirely shaped by historical fiction, starting with the American Girls series, which she has read and reread many times. That has been a jumping-off point for her interest in Native Americans and the Underground Railroad. She has just now developed an interest in Joy Hakim's *History of US* series, which we read together.

We travel somewhere at least eight times a year and make an effort to share the history of where we are with the children. They love stories involving children of any kind. We also tell family stories of the past, which are always a big hit. Movies are also a great way to engage the children in history, although it can be somewhat perilous because so many are historically inaccurate. —*Carolyn*, Pennsylvania

Genealogy

One natural outgrowth of personalizing history by emphasizing how people make it is to look at your own family to discover where its individuals fit in. Genealogy can be a great way to make history real for your kids by tying events to people they—to be perfectly corny about it—relate to. Knowing that millions of immigrants came to the United States in the early decades of the twentieth century is one thing, but knowing that your own grandparents or great-grandparents did so—and how and why they came—is another matter entirely.

One of the nice things about genealogy, too, is that it is a family matter. If you've got older relatives still living, they can be a terrific resource for learning about what life was like during the past few decades—how their lives differed from yours and your kids'. Try

Q: How do you find out about things you want to do or learn about?

CALEB (14): That's a good question. I get my answers from my two wonderful grandpas that know a lot about a lot of stuff. My mom and dad know a lot of stuff, too. I have a really smart family that can teach me a lot.

recording interviews with them, either in print or on audio or video-tape, or asking if they have scrapbooks they're willing to share; you may find that they're eager to share their views and experiences with you.

Living History

But maybe reading about their favorite historical period, or watching videos, or even talking directly with people who were there won't be enough for your kids. Maybe what they really want is to *live* their history. In that case, what you'll need is a bit of living history—what the professionals call "environmental living programs" (ELPs).

An ELP may run for a day only, for a twenty-four-hour overnight, or even for several days. Typically, participants will research a historical period, create an appropriate costume to wear, and adopt the persona of a historical character to impersonate during the ELP event. With most programs, the participants will perform at the historical site, in their historical personae, using period equipment and artifacts. In many cases, they will answer questions and demonstrate crafts (in character) for visitors to the site.

Check into historical monuments and parks to see whether they offer such programs. Some state or national parks have overnight programs they offer regularly to school groups. In such cases, your local homeschooling support group may want to form a class-sized group in order to participate. ELPs that offer programs to schools are often extremely popular and are booked as much as a year or two in advance, so it's best to allow plenty of time for planning.

Some historical sites offer programs especially for home-schoolers; they can range from admission discounts to full-fledged ELP events. Other sites may be more selective about allowing access to their artifacts, limiting their programs to individuals who go through a docent training program and commit to volunteering regularly at the site. Working as a docent can be a great experience; programs that are unwilling to accept kids, even teens, may be willing to work with them as part of a family group.

Another living history option is hobby reenactments. Different types of reenactments are popular in different parts of the country: Minutemen in New England, mountain men in the Intermountain West, wagon trains in the West. Civil War reenactment groups, while more numerous in the South, can be found throughout the country, as can members of the medieval/early Renaissance recreators of the Society for Creative Anachronism.

Travel

Travel can also be a great way to explore history. You can take a regional approach and simply visit interesting historical sites wherever you happen to spend your vacation.

This fall, we're going to a family wedding on the East Coast. We're going to take our first vacation in some time and go spend a week around Williamsburg and Jamestown. I think the boys will be taken with the living history stuff (something we've found worth looking for, since real people can be interacted with). —*Patrick*, California

My husband hates to fly but likes to travel, so we drive lots of places. We've been to Florida twice, and all up and down the West Coast. Having the kids actually see Fort Sumter or a cotton gin or try on a pioneer hat makes things more meaningful. Sarah, especially, can tie things in books to things she's seen. —*Ruth*, Montana

Some unschooling families prefer historically themed travel; they create a route based on a specific interest, such as the Revolutionary or Civil Wars or the Oregon Trail, and read ahead about the sights they plan to see. Others prefer to hit the trail first, and read related material while they're on the road or once they get home.

Putting It All Together

Few families stick to only one of these options in their approach to history. Most of us use most of them over the years, and with several different eras. Our kids' interests change as they grow older, and studying one area leads inevitably to at least six others they want to explore.

We were reading the "Little House on the Prairie" series, and had recently seen a program on the History Channel about the Oregon Trail and the whole westward movement. That soon turned into a major discovery fest! They made models of covered wagons and downloaded a list of supplies used at the time (and decided what they would have bought). We read books together, and that sparked more ideas. We began cooking pioneer meals and learning about the cowboys and what they did.

That pushed us into the world of folklore and tall tales. They learned about the real lives of Johnny (Appleseed) Chapman and Daniel Boone. They also learned about folk heroes such as Paul Bunyan and John Henry. Then they became interested in the American Indians after reading a book from the library. One day I was surprised to find a teepee (made of broomsticks and old sheets) in my living room! They played for days making bows and arrows, native headdresses, and feathers; they even cooked some Native American foods for dinner! They learned about tools they made and languages developed, and then checked out some historical videotapes from the library to learn about the Indians who lived in our area of California.

They began asking about the people in our family after we lost my grandfather in November. So we naturally started making a genealogical chart. The kids made a huge construction-paper tree, hung it, and began adding family members in branches to show what "side" they were on. We found that we are related to some historical figures, and we began studying them, too. We use the Internet, library, encyclopedias, and family members as resources. —*Laura Y.*, California

We learn a lot of history from our reading, both historical fiction and nonfiction. We also frequent museums. I've never found a history text that was interesting and presented an unbiased view. I read constantly and we always talk a lot about what we're reading. When our older daughters were interested in Helen Keller, we read her autobiography, a biography, the biography of her teacher, Annie Sullivan, the story of Laura Bridgeman (an earlier blind-deaf child whose training provided the framework for Helen's teaching), and the story of Louis Braille. We found samples of Braille writing and tried to feel the letters. Amie used to blindfold herself and stumble around the house bumping into things!

When they were fascinated with the story of the Underground Railroad, we read many books, again both fiction and nonfiction. The girls went outside at night and tried to find the North Star and to feel for moss on the north side of trees. When I wrote my little historical novel, they came with me while I did the research, accompanying me to the city archives, the Northwest Room of the main library, and several museums and historical sites. —*Terry*, British Columbia

History, when I was in school, was the most boring ordeal, because it was all political and military history. Yawn. Our approach to history starts in a very different place. We're all making history, all the time. Keeping records of what we do, what we see, what our lives are like leads us to be fascinated with things in the past. We love maps, and love to compare maps of the same place from different times. Graveyards are fascinating places to explore history; you can learn a lot by looking at the patterns of death. We travel quite a bit, and tend to explore historical stuff wherever we are. Genealogy makes it all very personal. Overall, I think we start from where we are, and then go back, looking to see how we got here.

I'm not at all concerned with there being gaps. History is all relative, anyway. It's personal. The stories we see are all slanted by who is doing the telling and why. The importance of any one event over another depends on your own beliefs. The important thing is to recognize that everything has a history, that many things that happen are in direct response to earlier events, and that you can make sense of the world if you look at its patterns.
—*Linda*, New York

Resources

Books

Carey, John, ed. *Eyewitness to History* (Avon Books, 1987). Carey has collected more than three hundred first-person accounts of events, both earthshaking and trivial, from over 2,500 years.

Cassidy, John. *Earthsearch: A Kids' Geography Museum in a Book* (Klutz Press, 1994). The Klutz folks tackle geography with their usual panache—and plenty of thought-provoking activities to interest both kids and adults.

Croom, Emily Anne. *Unpuzzling Your Past: A Basic Guide to Genealogy* (Betterway Publications, 1995). Croom's book is an unintimidating and straight-forward introduction to the process of collecting and preserving family history, with everything from where and how to look for information to deciphering unfamiliar handwriting styles.

Gonick, Larry. *The Cartoon History of the United States* (Harper Perennial, 1991).

Gonick, Larry. *The Cartoon History of the Universe/Volumes 1–7* (Doubleday, 1990).

Gonick, Larry. *The Cartoon History of the Universe II: From the Springtime of China to the Fall of Rome/Volumes 8–13* (Main Street Books, 1994). Gonick's histories take his usual funny and irreverent, but solid, approach to people and events.

Grun, Bernard. *The Timetables of History: A Horizontal Linkage of People and Events* (Simon & Schuster, 1991). Not only a useful reference, but great fun to browse through, this volume provides year-by-year information by category: history and politics; literature and theater; religion, philosophy, and learning; visual arts; music; science, technology, and growth; and daily life.

Hakim, Joy. *A History of US* (Oxford University Press, 1995). Hakim's ten-volume series is immensely popular among homeschoolers, and deservedly so. She is a terrific storyteller, and succeeds in making American history a product of the people who lived it. Each volume (written for ages eight through fourteen) includes a choice selection of books for further reading, including novels set in the period covered.

Kindersley, Barnabas and Anabel. *Children Just Like Me: A Unique Celebration of Children Around the World* (Dorling Kindersley, 1995). Each double-page spread in this delightful book focuses on specific children from a different country, with pictures and descriptions of their food, clothing, writing, and everyday life. The differences and the similarities among them are poignant and engrossing.

Lewis, Barbara A. *The Kid's Guide to Social Action* (Free Spirit Publishing, 1991). Lewis' book encourages a hands-on approach to learning about government and social change by getting personally involved; plenty of ideas for effective action.

Loewen, James W. *Lies My Teacher Told Me: Everything Your American History Textbook Got Wrong* (Simon & Schuster/Touchstone, 1996). Fascinating look at American history textbooks' failure both to teach good history and to explain why it matters. Loewen's book may surprise even those who believe they are knowledgeable about American history.

Menzel, Peter. *Material World: A Global Family Portrait* (Sierra Club Books, 1994). This extraordinary book is based on a simple idea: find a statistically "average" family for each of thirty different countries throughout the world, and photograph them, with all of their worldly goods, in front of their dwelling. The results are breathtaking—a stunning illustration of the reality and the humanity behind the statistics. A sequel of sorts, *Women in the Material World,* is also available.

Shoumatoff, Alex. *The Mountain of Names* (Simon & Schuster, 1985). Based on a *New Yorker* article of the same title, Shoumatoff's book is a marvelous discussion of kinship and family relationships and how they intertwine through history. His "mountain of names" is both figurative and a reference to the Granite Mountain Vault, the Mormons' repository for their genealogical archives.

Tuchman, Barbara. *Practicing History: Selected Essays* (Ballantine Books, 1982). Tuchman, one of the best modern writers of historical narrative, discusses in these essays the exacting work of writing history, and the choices that tellers of history must make in the course of constructing their stories.

Weitzman, David L. *My Backyard History Book* (Little, Brown & Co., 1975). Another book in the terrific Brown Paper School Book series, this volume encourages kids to look at home, at their family, and at their neighborhood for the history they can find all around them.

Wolfman, Ira. *Do People Grow on Family Trees? Genealogy for Kids & Other Beginners* (Workman Publishing, 1991). Produced in association with the Statue of Liberty–Ellis Island Foundation, this friendly introduction to genealogy includes considerable material on the American immigrant experience.

Zinn, Howard. *A People's History of the United States: 1492–Present* (Harper Perennial, 1995). Along with Loewen's book, this is a great antidote to traditional American history textbooks. Zinn looks at events from the perspective of the people affected by them, rather than constantly from the view of the more conventionally chosen historical figures.

Organizations

Cobblestone Publishing Company, 7 School Street, Peterborough, NH 03458; 800-821-0115 or 603-924-7209. Cobblestone publishes several magazines for ages nine through fourteen, including *Cobblestone,* on American history; *Faces,* on world cultures; and *Calliope,* on world history.

National Geographic Society, 1145 17th Street NW, Washington, DC 20036-4688; 800-647-5463; www.nationalgeographic.com. The Society's magazines (*National Geographic* and *National Geographic World*) are their most familiar products, but they also publish terrific maps, atlases, and other books.

Society for Creative Anachronism, P.O. Box 360789, Milpitas, CA 95036-0789; 800-789-7486; www.sca.org. The SCA specializes in selective recreation of aspects of the European High Middle Ages, including dance, calligraphy, martial arts, cooking, metalwork, stained glass, costuming, literature, and more. A great resource for anyone fascinated by that historical period.

U.S. Census Bureau. The Census Bureau maintains an interesting Web site (www.census.gov) full of demographic and economic information about the United States and other countries.

CHAPTER NINE

The Arts

RARE IS THE preschooler who is not an avid artist of one kind or another. We Americans encourage our young children to play around with paper and crayons. Some of us even have the patience to deal with the aftermath of their playing around with scissors and paints, too. From the time when they can first hold a crayon, kids almost constantly draw pictures for us, bang rhythmically on pots and pans in lieu of "real" drums, and present energetic—if often incomprehensible—theatrical performances for anyone within earshot. Many parents even use the presence of art and music materials and activities as one criterion for determining the quality of a preschool for their children.

But something happens to most of these budding artists in formal educational settings. Art becomes a once-a-week school subject—good for developing fine motor skills and learning color names—and all that artistic energy is redirected into group craft projects. In the interests of keeping things reasonably organized and uncomplicated, art becomes a matter of photocopied color-cut-and-paste projects, and every kid's work, within the limited variation of neatness in coloring and cutting, looks pretty much like every other kid's. For most kids, art becomes something that requires vastly more "talent" than they possess—something out of their reach.

The process is much the same for other areas of the arts. The dedicated and exuberant singer, hummer, or pot-banger learns to subdue her music, and playacting becomes something that "little kids" do. Except for those few "talented" individuals, music and theater become things to listen to or see performances of, not things for everyone to do.

Without the demands on their time that their schooled peers have, unschooled kids tend to continue with the arts activities they enjoy long after traditional school age.

They both love to draw and paint. My wife tends to introduce the crafts projects, but the boys then demand them. Performing? Well, other than incredible histrionic productions (great theater value), they've been taken with puppets recently, and have enjoyed watching and putting on some puppet theater. —*Patrick,* California

We have a piano, and the kids spend time "composing" their own songs. They don't write them down, but they do remember them and play them often. We have a couple of piano books (and two recorders) for them to use at will. They both draw and create lots of craft projects. —*Andrea, Nevada*

We do a lot of finger painting, clay, Play-Doh, watercolor, and oil pastel artwork in our house. My husband has a natural talent for drawing, and the kids pick up on that and try to imitate his skills. We do a lot of crafts and activities like ceramics, painted "stained" glass projects, woodworking, collages, and 3-D art on a daily basis. The children are very good at expressing themselves in a variety of ways. —*Laura Y.,* California

Not too surprisingly, given our aversion to structured lessons in general, unschoolers tend to avoid formal arts instruction as well. All too often, we find, children's programs in art are too prescriptive, too product-oriented to hold our kids' attention for very long.

Elisabeth draws and paints the way I used to read as a child—almost compulsively—and since neither I nor my husband are particularly skilled or interested in art, she's tried a few art classes. The first was at what looked like a wonderful kids' art center, with plenty of good-quality paints and clay, and encouraging instructors. For the first couple of weeks, she was thrilled; she was learning new techniques that enabled her to do some great-looking pieces. The problem was that the techniques were developed by everyone in the class doing exactly the same piece; then the next week, they'd all learn another technique by making another piece to take home and show their parents. There was never any opportunity to try the new skills with her own ideas, and she got so stressed and discouraged at the classes that she almost completely quit doing any drawing or painting at home.

The next place we found was a bit better, but went too far to the opposite extreme. It had more of a studio atmosphere, where she got to work on her own ideas, but she didn't get much help learning new techniques, and didn't really know enough yet to be able to ask for what she needed. Since then, she's decided she's better off working on her own for the time being. She pores over books and illustrations by artists she likes, and attempts to copy work she admires, and refers to books on technique. We're hoping one day to find someone she can work with, but since she's got fairly definite ideas now about what kind of help she wants, we're taking our time finding the right mentor. —*Ann, California*

What works for most of us is to let our children experiment with the arts—singing for the pure fun of it, drawing, painting, dancing, playacting, sculpture and other three-dimensional work, and playing with drums, keyboards, or other musical instruments. A bit of experience working in various media makes visits to museums and galleries, to theaters and other performing arts venues, all the more meaningful; we and our kids can begin to grasp the skills, effort, and discipline that go into creating such productions. Over time, our kids discover what they enjoy and what they are good at. Some eventually reach the point where they want to learn more, and ask for formal music lessons or art instruction, or perhaps to join some sort of performing group. A few find their intense interests developing into a vocation. Others are simply content to have found hobbies they can enjoy for years.

> What works for most of us is to let our children experiment with the arts—singing for the pure fun of it, drawing, painting, dancing, play-acting, sculpture and other three-dimensional work, and playing with drums, keyboards, or other musical instruments.

My husband and his parents are all artists. When Dan and I first discussed keeping our kids out of school, I suggested that they could go to school for some activities like art. "No way," he said. He thinks art is one of the main reasons to keep kids out of school. He still remembers being told by his art teacher that his picture was wrong because he put purple in his trees. He's never quite gotten over that. He often points out trees with purple tints in their leaves.

We have all kinds of art supplies at home, and the kids are welcome to use them whenever they like. They both paint and draw and make all kinds of crafts like textiles and whittling. They both weave and crochet and do leather work and bead work and pottery. They can't remember a time when they weren't doing arts and crafts. I think they're very artistic.

They also both take piano, and Jordan has several years of violin and ballet. Also, they both like to sing in the children's choir at church, and Jordan goes to the school for choir.

We live in a small town that has a small, private four-year college, so they've been going to concerts, recitals, art shows, plays, and operas since they were born. They don't always want to go, but they usually end up liking the performances. We attend at least one college performance a week, I'd guess. I think it's been wonderful for the kids, and of course I enjoy it, too.

Oh, and Jordan took art lessons from Dan's mom once a week all last fall. It was as much a chance for them to spend time together as an art lesson, but Jordan came home with some beautiful work she'd done.

Both kids have made Christmas presents for the entire extended family since they can remember. I helped them when they were very young, two to five, but since then they've been choosing their own projects and completing the gifts entirely on their own. They've wood-burned wooden spoons, woven pot holders, crocheted bags, painted bookmarks, designed jewelry, and baked treats. They sometimes make their own wrapping paper and note cards. It's all self-initiated. —*Susan,* Iowa

We've done as much hands-on art and music as is feasible on a limited budget. We have lots of arts and crafts supplies, and Chase has taken an occasional Parks-and-Rec-type art course. We've visited a few art museums and viewed fine arts as they exist in the community. Music is on in our house most of the time—all kinds of music (except opera and country!). The kids have also had the chance to play drums, keyboard, recorder, guitar, harmonica, flute, and other homemade instruments at will. Neither child has taken formal music lessons, although I fill them in on whatever music theory they need in order to do what they want to, like chord songs on the guitar, etc. —*Carol,* Florida

Arts. Stay out! Let your kids do whatever they want and don't act like they will never learn how to draw, paint, etc. without instruction. Do not worry whether they can play some instrument if all they like to do is scribble. Kids are naturally creative, and if you leave them to their own devices you will be amazed at what they will do. Just be sure to have all sorts of supplies handy! —*Chase,* Florida

We have a piano and recorders (as well as violin, cello, and flute) accessible to the children—and they do doodle on them. We also sing in the car as a family, and listen to classical, folk, and children's music. For a while, the children were in a German-language children's choir that I thought was great, but they hated it. So we aren't doing that anymore. However, my daughter is now in two drama groups, one of which includes singing and dancing along with the drama.

I think that, beyond the appreciation the children get for a performing art, the act of actually performing is important. When the children are young, I look for performing groups in which they can be one of the gang on stage. As their abilities and confidence grow, I like to see little solos. However, it is very important to make it clear that their worth is not dependent on a particular performance or on their talents, but instead on the effect they have on those around them.

I am still the one to initiate all these activities. Since we don't do much of this at home, the children don't know enough about them to be interested. They are still good sports, though, and try what I suggest, but I will not push it if they develop a real dislike of it. I've seen too many people learn to hate music by being forced into piano or violin lessons. —*Carolyn*, Pennslyvania

We all have a varied interest in music, so the kids have lots of opportunities to listen to different types. They really don't have favorite music types; once when Ally was asked by a friend what kind of music she liked, she said anything but country and rap. Both kids are rather shy performers. They will playact together, but they won't let me or Dave see their creations, and they wouldn't do it in front of a group. Ally has even specifically told us that if she has to perform on stage as part of dance lessons she doesn't want to go. —*Marianne*, Arizona

Now you're in our area! My husband is a professional musician, I write and illustrate children's books, my father was a sculptor, and Jack's parents are both musicians. I believe in providing children with the raw materials for creative expression and letting them explore freely. We have always had a good selection of children's music (and our own interests in classical and

Q: Some critics of unschooling say that it can't work because kids allowed to control their own learning won't do difficult things or things they dislike. Do you agree with this?

CHASE (18): I think that every child has such a need to be curious and to learn that, if left alone, they will learn many a difficult thing, even things they dislike. Do you think learning how to walk and talk was easy?

For instance, I dislike fixing the things that fall apart around the house or having to board up the house because a hurricane's coming. But I have to do these things anyway; I don't really have a choice, in that it's easier to fix them now than pay the consequences later. Sure there are lots of things that are hard to learn, but that doesn't mean you don't want to learn them with just as much intensity. And after you learn them, they are so much sweeter than if they came to you easily.

Personally, I think the critics of unschooling do not trust themselves to do the things they do not like without someone hitting them over the head with it, and so of course they can't imagine how it could possibly be any different. And in some ways, those are the people who need unschooling the most.

folk and jazz are well represented!), and a piano and simple instruments like recorders, rhythm instruments, and folk harp available. We sing a lot. I often put on music for the little ones to dance to. When they were about three, they enjoyed a weekly Orff-Kodaly class. There are plenty of art supplies for painting, drawing, collage, modeling, and crafts. We used to act out fairy tales—with hilarious results. (You should have seen our dog playing the part of the Big Bad Wolf!) As the girls got older, they asked for lessons in such things as ballet, pottery, piano, voice, choir, violin, drama, and art. Their artistic passions know no bounds!

Tessa is now taking ballet, violin, and Bach choir. In the summers she is particularly busy. The past two summers she has done a two-week choir camp (she's doing it again in one week; she loves it so much that she wouldn't miss it!), ballet summer school, and a week-long art camp on a farm (wonderful experience!). This year she's going to do a week of "Summer Strings" music camp that includes country dancing and ensemble playing. She gets her fill of getting up early during the summer, and by August says that she can't wait for school to start so she can sleep in!
—*Terry*, British Columbia

Supplies

The actual mix of supplies you have around the house for your kids to use is not crucial, and it will vary, of course, depending on their ages and interests. You'll find that odds and ends of all sorts will be useful: fabric and wood scraps, "craft" sticks (popsicle sticks), yarn, paints and brushes of all kinds, musical instruments, old clothes for costumes, socks for puppets, and so on. One caveat, though: you will probably find that your kids will be much happier with real, professional art supplies than with the sort packaged especially for children.

The best investment I made was a $200 set of professional marker pens. They have been through two children and are still used almost daily after six

years. Good art materials mean that the kids don't get disappointed in their art because of difficulty with their paints or whatever. You can buy really horrid watercolors that have very little pigment and are very hard. I have let the kids use my tube watercolors, starting out with only a couple of colors—such as red and blue and turquoise—chosen so they wouldn't all make brown when they ran together. Mostly though, just by having things around, their creativity has shone through. My youngest, at age five, made puppets with a friend for over a year; he took card stock, drew and colored the figures with markers, cut them out, and taped them to popsicle sticks. They performed wonderful plays. I still have boxes of those puppets!
—*Jill, California*

It doesn't seem to matter how carefully or how many times I explain to all the relatives who like to get art supplies for my kids for Christmas and birthday presents that we don't need yet another of those crummy kids' art sets, with the waxy crayons, brittle colored pencils, flaky watercolor pans, and stiff brushes that shed hair all over paintings. The aunts and uncles and grandparents see all those pretty colors arranged in appealing rainbow patterns, and think what a good bargain the package is. But it's been so long since they've done any artwork of their own (if they ever did) that they don't realize how awful that stuff is to work with. The colors are pale or just weird, the crayons and pencils break; it's practically guaranteed to discourage anybody who tries to use them. It's much better to spend the money for really good materials. You may not get as many items, but what you get will be used more, and more effectively and enjoyably, too.
—*Ann, California*

Lessons

One aspect of working in the arts that always comes up in discussions among unschoolers is the decisions to be made about lessons—specifically, once your child has started lessons, what role do you as a parent play? Is it your job to enforce the suggested practice your child has supposedly committed to? What if your child decides she is no longer interested in the lessons?

As always, the answers will depend on the particulars of your situation, but it's important to be aware of some of the issues that inevitably arise. Some parents talk with their kids ahead of time about what's expected: how much practice is required or suggested, whether the child wants to be reminded about practice or left to decide for herself, whether consequences for not practicing will be imposed by the parent or left as a matter between the child and her teacher.

The decision about when to quit lessons can be a complicated one. Your child may simply lose interest in painting or ballet or piano, or she might have a problem with the teacher's style. In most cases, talking it over with your child is important; you don't want her just dropping lessons because she has one or two bad days, but neither do you want her plodding on through something she's seriously no longer interested in simply because she's supposed to finish what she starts.

For many older children, deciding to drop a class can be a difficult experience. The child who has studied piano and ballet for several years each, for instance, may reach a point at which continuing with either requires a commitment that makes continuing the other impossible. Letting go of one may not be easy. It is important to listen carefully to your child, to help her evaluate the alternatives, and to make sure she doesn't base her decisions on others' wishes for her instead of her own best interests. Fortunately, because of their experience with choosing and evaluating their own learning activities, unschoolers usually find themselves well prepared to make such potentially life-changing decisions.

In a few cases, a child's decision to drop lessons after several years can be upsetting to the parents. You may think of all the money you've spent on lessons and supplies, and of how good your child is at what she does. "How could she give that up after all we've put into it all these years?" But your child may think, "I've done this now; I've had enough, and now I'm ready to try other things." It may help to consider how you would view a similar decision by an adult friend: if it's reasonable for your friend to choose another way to spend her time and energy or just to take a break, is it any less reasonable a decision for your child to make? After all, those years of lessons and practice have not really been wasted; in addition to a lot of technique, your child has learned about discipline, self-control, perseverance, and how to achieve her goals. Those are skills and qualities that will help her in whatever she decides to do in the future.

Resources

Books

Blood, Peter, and Annie Patterson, eds. *Rise Up Singing: The Group Singing Songbook* (Sing Out! Publications, 1992). This collection of hundreds of song lyrics (and chord patterns for guitar accompaniment) includes Broadway and popular songs but emphasizes folk songs; includes variations on traditional lyrics for many songs.

Brookes, Mona. *Drawing with Children* (Jeremy P. Tarcher, 1986).

Brookes, Mona. *Drawing for Older Children & Teens* (Jeremy P. Tarcher, 1991). Brookes offers accessible techniques for anyone interested in learning to draw what they see.

Edwards, Betty. *Drawing on the Right Side of the Brain: A Course in Enhancing Creativity and Artistic Confidence* (Jeremy P. Tarcher, 1979). Edwards' presentation of basic ideas, such as proportion and perspective, also provides many ideas to help any potential artist become less self-conscious and more confident about her skills.

Haab, Sherri, and Laura Torres. *The Incredible Clay Book* (Klutz Press, 1994). You'll be amazed at what you can create with the techniques presented in this book and the polymer clay included; another of the wonderful Klutz activity books for all ages.

Holt, John. *Never Too Late: My Musical Life Story* (Addison-Wesley Publishing Co., 1991). Holt's account of taking up the cello at middle age is encouraging to anyone learning music on their own.

Hurd, Thacher and John Cassidy. *Watercolor for the Artistically Undiscovered* (Klutz Press, 1992). The bright, clear watercolor paints included with this book make your work look almost as good as Hurd's examples in this no-wrong-way-to-paint guide.

Judy, Stephanie. *Making Music for the Joy of It: Enhancing Creativity, Skills, and Musical Confidence* (Jeremy P. Tarcher, Inc., 1990). Judy is full of ideas for learning music, no matter what level you seek to pursue; plenty of advice for practicing on your own, playing along with others, and venturing into performing.

Kohl, Herbert. *Making Theater: Developing Plays with Young People* (Teachers & Writers Collaborative, 1988). This little book is full of suggestions for helping kids with theater. Includes lots of material on adapting traditional stories to suit a particular group of performers, improvisation, and writing original pieces.

Wilson, Frank R. *Tone Deaf & All Thumbs: An Invitation to Music-Making* (Vintage Books, 1987). Wilson, a neurology professor and amateur musician, discusses how the brain works when we hear and when we create music, and agrees with Holt that it is indeed "never too late" to learn music.

Catalogs

Homespun Music Tapes, Box 694, Woodstock, NY 12498. Homespun sells excellent instructional tapes for guitar, fiddle, piano, and other instruments; for beginning to advanced students.

Lark in the Morning, P.O. Box 1176, Mendocino, CA 95460; 707-964-5569; www.larkinam.com. If it's played somewhere in the world, Lark in the Morning can probably get one for you. This incredible catalog of all kinds of unusual musical instruments is an education in itself; also has a huge selection of music books and recordings.

Music for Little People, P.O. Box 1460, Redway, CA 95560; 800-727-2233. This terrific catalog offers an interesting selection of recorded music in a variety of genres (folk, world, classical), along with lots of kid-sized musical instruments.

CHAPTER TEN

Changes As Kids Grow Older

I T'S INEVITABLE: JUST when you think you finally have your kids and your lives all figured out, all set for everything to go smoothly for months or maybe even years, your children change on you. Suddenly the help they welcomed from you yesterday is an unasked-for intrusion. Or things they were perfectly content to do on their own last week they suddenly and desperately need assistance with. The child who happily unschooled for years suddenly begins to wonder if she isn't just a bit too odd for "normal" society, or her younger brother abruptly decides he's been learning to program in C++ all wrong and needs a knowledgeable mentor immediately.

How do you figure out how much help to give your kids when the amount and kind of help they want changes all the time?

Helping kids to become independent learners is one of the hardest tasks in homeschooling. Each child is different and seems to change constantly with age. What was helpful one year is seen as pushy the next. Or

I hear the cry "You didn't help me enough!" I try to help as much as I'm wanted, and I probably err on the side of not helping when I should. With unschooling, it's hard to know how much is my responsibility and how much belongs to the kids. Take the arts, for example: Is it my job to provide an encompassing range of artistic opportunities for them to choose from, or do I wait until they express an interest in some particular area?

Andy just asked yesterday about college. He has always been a bit of a worrier. He likes to know what is happening, and really hates changes or unexpected events. A routine and patterns are very important to him. He's already looking for a house site to build his own house on. The redeeming grace is that once he has a plan, he feels secure and can go on with things, even if later the plan proves unworkable and circumstances change. I sincerely doubt that the house site he picks at twelve will be where he lives at twenty-five, but having thought about it, he can now move on to worry about other things.

Sarah also makes plans, but hers are much more imaginary. She doesn't seem to worry about the future. At nine, college and adult life are very distant to her and she tries on different adult roles (teacher, vet, nurse, astronaut, cook, mother) as often as she changes clothes—three or four times a day. At the moment, very much to my liberated-female chagrin, she seems to lean toward very traditionally female roles. However, she does build things with my husband and enjoys getting wet, muddy, and dirty.
—*Ruth*, Montana

The first crack of independence comes when they begin to read things you haven't the time or inclination to read. The hardest thing has always been to sit on my hands and keep my mouth shut, to not do or interfere or make suggestions—unless asked, unless invited to do so. —*Cindy*, Wisconsin

Children can use all the help you can give them—when they ask for it. Otherwise we can really get in the way. The trick for me is knowing when they are asking for help.

Sometimes it is as obvious as a request for help or a question. Sometimes (but not always), a "Mommy, I'm bored" is a request for help. Then we might try something brand-new or go to a new place. Sometimes we need to let the boredom happen, though, since it, too, is a learning experience.

Sometimes the request comes as an obsession with something. Then I try to support their interest and perhaps introduce something similar or related to it. For example, my son was terrifically interested in the *Star Trek* TV shows. So I borrowed the *Star Trek Omnipedia* CD-ROM from the library so he could learn about all the gory details of the starship. I was handy for all the vocabulary questions that crop up from a six-year-old struggling with an adult computer program. The program also contained video clips of special effects from the shows that he could run over and over again. At that point, it was easy to interest him in special effects, and we hauled out our video camera so we could do some of our own experiments.

The most subtle requests for help come when they are acting out or unhappy. This is the most difficult to know what to do with, especially since the child has no idea what they need, either. We try to deal with this by examining our current activities and tweaking them until we feel better.

Most of these issues crop up for any parent. Just when we think we've figured the kids out, they grow some more and change. As unschoolers, though, we have to deal with these issues from hour to hour, and can't ignore or defer them as some parents can. —*Carolyn*, Pennslyvania

The older they get, the less direct help they need from me—the more I am truly just a resource for them. I always try to step back and wait to be asked for help. Of course, sometimes I'm better at that than other times! Keeping up with their changing needs isn't that difficult, because I am with them and aware of these changes, so it just flows from living together.

Chase is in the throes of considering the issues of college, jobs, her place in life, etc. In typical unschooling fashion, she is questioning everything. I hope I have no preconceived notion of when she will move on to the next phase in her life or what form that phase will take (although her dad assumes it will be college). She has an SAT preparation guide and has done the verbal half of it. She'll tackle the math

when she decides it's necessary; it's not her favorite topic. I suspect her dad wishes I would push her more on these issues, but it doesn't make any sense to me to do that. We are spending literally hours a week discussing those growing-up, "Who am I?" issues. I agree with Mary Pipher, in *Reviving Ophelia*, that teenagers take more of our time than toddlers. I am grateful to have the time to do so, even though it isn't always easy for me to have my choices so closely examined as well. I have total confidence that she will find her own way with great style and energy.
—*Carol*, Florida

My mom has not really been that involved in the actual pursuit of knowledge with me for a long time. Not that she doesn't know what I am doing; she does, because I talk about it and use her to bounce ideas off. And by talking to her I can start digesting and formulating my own ideas about any given subject. But pretty much she just leaves me alone and sits back and listens to me talk and talk and talk.

I have always preferred to learn new things by myself when there is no one to watch me, and then when I have perfected it to my satisfaction, I will share it with the rest of the world. As far as life when I don't live with my parents anymore, I know I will do what I am supposed to do, and I will know when I am supposed to know, and not before. —*Chase*, Florida

We have found, over the years, that an independent learner needs very little help. Of course, this means that we can't get antsy when our teens still don't seem to be doing anything that *looks* like school! We're so used to the school picture of what learning looks like that we can't recognize the learning that goes on when we read a book, discuss politics, or figure out our finances. I'm much more confident now that I have two who have gone on to college and university after our casual approach to schooling.

I think the time to step in and help is when we're asked for help. We might suggest that this would be a good time to work on a particular subject that we think they'll need, but we can only suggest; they are free to

Q: Do you worry sometimes about being different from most other kids?

CHASE (18): As a kid and an adolescent, I would often worry about always being different from other kids. It is human nature to want to fit in and be liked. But I learned the hard way that, no matter what you do, you can never truly fit in with something fake or if you change yourself to fit in. The only way to fit in is to be yourself and not worry about whether or not you do fit in. But then I would never fit in with most people anyway, even if I did go to school. I am just too weird, I suppose. But then I always take that as being a compliment, and being on the outside has its advantages. But yes, we all sometimes want to fit in—no matter how old and wise we are.

refuse (and frequently do!). I think that to have a good, respectful relationship with our teens we need to be sensitive to their right to choose what they are learning and how they want to pursue it. The best way to keep up with changing needs is to stand back and let them direct themselves. Just as we found that the best way to know when a child is ready for toilet training is to relax and watch the child's readiness, we do better to let our teens lead the way in their own education. —*Terry*, British Columbia

The trick is to continue to listen to your children as they grow older, and keep helping them find the resources they need for what they want to learn and do. Gradually, you'll find them doing more of the work themselves, and your own role will become more that of advisor or even colleague as they get ready to move out on their own.

Going to School

Somewhere around ages twelve to fourteen, quite a few unschooled kids start wondering about school, about what they've opted out of. They begin to wonder whether they could handle the work schoolkids their age are expected to handle, and they start to consider whether they want to participate in the social and other extracurricular activities centered around school.

For some of these kids, arranging for them to spend a day or a week in a classroom is enough to satisfy their curiosity. They may enjoy the novelty while it lasts, but decide that the structured day and predetermined course of study is not for them, and choose to continue homeschooling. Others may decide that school is how they want to learn; they may stay for a term or a whole year and then return to unschooling, or they may opt to remain in school through graduation. (A few even treat a limited stretch in school as a kind of anthropological field study, looking at the dynamics of group behavior.) Whichever choice they make, the decision is usually not an easy one, and they (and you) will probably consider and reconsider the consequences for months.

The year Elisabeth turned twelve was hard for her. Several of her friends who homeschooled decided to go to school, which pretty well ended the friendships. They no longer had as much time to spend with her as they once had, and when they did manage to get together, Elisabeth found she no longer had much in common with them. It was a real disappointment to her, not just because she lost the friends, but because she had thought there was more to the friendships than turned out to be the case. She considered—for maybe five minutes—trying school herself, but decided that the odds of finding good friends weren't high enough to offset all the disadvantages of living and learning to someone else's schedule.
—*Ann, California*

Going to school was a bit tough to adjust to, mostly in terms of time—not just having to be there at certain times every day, but home time. I have to take a lot of stuff home and I don't have as much time as I'd like for things I want to do.

One big difference I see between myself and other kids at school is that I approach work differently. They seem to have a "let's get it over with and go home" attitude, and I sort of say "Enjoy yourself, learn, and relax." I'm doing pretty well with that view, too (3.71 grade point average, no honors or AP classes). I think homeschooling gave me that attitude—"learning should entertain"—in a different way than other kids. I feel it's one's own obligation to make one's learning entertaining, and some people rely on the teacher for entertainment, which generally gets the teacher fairly ticked off (and quickly).

Going to school does tend to make me less tolerant of my siblings, because I have more things to do and their concerns and arguments with me seem utterly trivial, which my parents don't seem to understand too well. Given a choice, though, I would definitely keep my life the way it has been. I have seen many people who went to schools all their K–8 years, and are utterly miserable here. Plus, I like some of the teachers and I am determined to make the most of my sojourn here. —*Sean,* California

The computer is sure lonely having Sean in school after so many years out. It took the rest of the kids several months to remember that Sean was off at school as we pursued our lives; they kept asking where he was. Sean was *ready* to be out of the house and leading a life separate from us. The first few weeks, he was very kind to all of us as he finally started appreciating the difference in acceptance between school and home.

I really feared he would have trouble keeping up with seven different classes and all the work that entailed. But he loves mastering the external challenge, and for the most part is willing to play the game of school. He has had trouble managing his time efficiently and getting to the schoolwork that he likes least. All his reading has made him an interesting and interested student. He already knows a lot and loves learning more. He loves to challenge his teachers (in a positive way) and stretch their learning, too.

Although Sean is happy, the rest of us are miserable. We hate living by the school schedule. Sean's school wants him there and is not at all interested in the idea of family time. We can't just pick up and go anymore. We have to plan around the school as if it were another member of the family. The worst is that Sean has bought in and never wants to miss school. And the whole thing about having to be a school parent and join the community of the school. I want to pick my own communities! And having to care about grades is another peeve.

Would we homeschool Sean again if we had it to do over? Absolutely! Sean would have been hammered in grade school for being himself. Since he has had nothing but time to grow into his skin, he is happy with who he is. He doesn't apologize for being himself and feels no need to conform to the wishes of others. Also, he would have been bored to tears in a conventional setting. I am very happy we have homeschooled, and only wish it could have lasted longer. —*Melissa, California*

> Having one child go off to school can mean major adjustments for the entire family. School means adjusting to a new schedule, to the demands of homework and extracurricular activities, to different ways of thinking about learning. Parents and siblings both have to adjust not only to the school student's absence during the day, but to his increased focus on school and away from the family.

As Melissa and Sean illustrate, having one child go off to school can mean major adjustments for the entire family. School means adjusting to a new schedule, to the demands of homework and extracurricular activities, to different ways of thinking about learning. Parents and siblings both have to adjust not only to the school student's absence during the day, but to his increased focus on school and away from the family.

Most unschoolers who attend school seem to do well both academically and socially, though sometimes after an initial adjustment period. One factor that seems to contribute to their success is the knowledge that they are there because they want to be, and that they know there are other educational options still available if they decide they want them.

Getting Ready for Life on Their Own

For unschoolers, the break between adolescence and adulthood—between life largely supervised by others and life on their own—is not as abrupt as many traditional high school graduates find it to be.

For unschoolers, the break between adolescence and adulthood—between life largely supervised by others and life on their own—is not as abrupt as many traditional high school graduates find it to be. They've been making many of their own decisions for several years, gradually becoming more and more independent. Many begin taking a course or two in particular subjects of interest at local community colleges at fifteen or sixteen, and already have a good idea of what college-level work entails. They are in a better position than many of their schooled peers to decide whether they want to pursue a college education immediately, delay it for a while in favor of travel or work, or choose some sort of technical or other specialized training.

A big advantage for homeschooling teens is that they are already part of the real world, not shut away in an artificial environment for most of their time. They learn to direct themselves, not to sit back and wait to be told what to do.

When our children were of an age to work, they started with baby-sitting. Amie started a birthday party service when she was about fifteen. She would dress as a clown and go to children's birthday parties and play a variety of games with the children and do face painting. This was popular, and made much better money than baby-sitting! She has still done the occasional birthday party even now, to supplement her income while she is a student. She also volunteered at the local cable television studio.

Anika has worked as a teacher's helper and then teaching preschool dance and drama classes for Parks and Recreation. She has also volunteered with "Leisure Link," another Parks and Rec program that finds volunteer buddies for special-needs people trying to integrate into the community. This has been very rewarding for her.

Tessa, at eleven, has just started to do a little baby-sitting as a mother's helper (meaning that she plays with the children while their mother is still at home getting work done on her home business—I wouldn't want her baby-sitting alone in a home this young!), and she volunteers helping with the preschool classes at her ballet studio.

All of these experiences do more than just give them good pocket money. They have helped prepare them for work, for independence, and for helping others. They have done this very much on their own, without any push from us. —*Terry*, British Columbia

There are a few basic steps your teen should probably take to keep all their options open for the future:

- Get familiar with the standardized tests used for college admissions (mainly the PSAT/NMSQT, SAT, and ACT). There are numerous test-preparation books available, including College Board editions of complete examinations used in previous years. Even if your child ultimately decides not to go to college, standardized tests are so ubiquitous in our society these days that knowing something about them will pay off.

- Learn about college admissions and financial aid at least a couple of years before you need to. Having some idea of the requirements for both will make acquiring the documents and other material you'll need an easier and less stressful process than if you wait until the last minute.

- Start assembling material to describe and document your skills, interests, and accomplishments. This could take the form of a portfolio, journal entries, letters of recommendation from mentors or other people you've worked for or with, transcripts of community college or other formal course-work, or a functional resume, among many possibilities.

Resources

Bear, John, and Mariah Bear. *Bear's Guide to Earning College Degrees Nontraditionally* (C & B Publishing, 1996). The Bears, father and daughter, provide advice on learning through correspondence and other alternative programs. Includes extensive listings of schools that offer such programs, and some fairly tart advice about diploma mills.

Boldt, Laurence G. (Penguin Books, 1993). *Zen and the Art of Making a Living: A Practical Guide to Creative Career Design* (Penguin Books, 1993). Boldt's is one of the better "career" guides available, including lots of information about different kinds of businesses and organizations, and how to figure out what kind of work you want.

Cohen, Cafi. *And What About College?* (Holt Associates, 1997). Cohen describes the process her kids used in applying to and being admitted to college. Includes a procedure for creating transcripts from less formal educational experiences.

Grand, Gail L. *Free (and Almost Free) Adventures for Teenagers* (John Wiley & Sons, 1995). Grand's book provides extensive listings of formal academic programs open to teens throughout the United States at no cost.

Gross, Ronald. *The Independent Scholar's Handbook* (Ten Speed Press, 1993). Gross offers plenty of solid advice about delving into any subject, and about finding others in the field to share information and experience with.

Hayes, Charles D. *Proving You're Qualified: Strategies for Competent People without College Degrees* (Autodidactic Press, 1995). Hayes talks about creeping credentialism, why employers and others increasingly rely on paper qualifications, and how self-taught individuals can focus attention on their actual skills.

Kimeldorf, Martin. *Creating Portfolios: For Success in School, Work, and Life* (Free Spirit Publishing, 1994). Kimeldorf offers solid advice on not only what to include in a portfolio, but why and how to present material for different purposes.

Llewellyn, Grace. *Real Lives: Eleven Teenagers Who Don't Go to School* (Lowry House, 1993). The teens who write about their lives in this collection of essays offer plenty of ideas for making the transition from childhood to life as an adult.

An Unschooling Week Three

Susan (Iowa) does not keep any formal records of her children's daily life, but recorded the family's activities for a week to give an idea of what that life is like: "I'm at work outside the home eight hours a day. (I would prefer to be home every day, even though I like my job, but I have to be satisfied with the fact that I was home with Caleb and Jordan until they were about seven and ten. I'll be working outside the home from now on, probably.) When I'm home we tend to work together on cleaning, organizing, and restoring the house, and we spend more time on playing games together and working on projects of all kinds."

SUNDAY:

- Sometimes we go to church on Sunday morning and sometimes we don't. The kids really liked their children's classes up until this year. They have very teacher-type adults leading their classes now, and their enthusiasm has waned considerably. Caleb's reading has improved by leaps and bounds in the past two years, but he still dislikes being required to read aloud in a group of his peers. He also is extremely sensitive about his handwriting and spelling. His current teacher typically introduces a topic and then requires the students to write down their thoughts concerning it. Then she has them exchange papers and read what each other has written. Caleb is my social child and absolutely loves going to church to be with his friends,

(continues)

163

but he has struggled with his dislike of this class for several weeks and has decided not to go anymore. Oh, well, I could have volunteered to teach their class myself and didn't, so I'm not likely to complain. We'll just have to hope for a different teacher next year. Every other kid in the class goes to school five days a week. It seems really sad to me that Sunday school is modeled on the same boring tasks.

- If we don't go to church, we hang out together at home. We generally play games or work on some project on our hundred-year-old house. This particular Sunday, Dan and I hung an antique general store shelf on the wall in the study. Dan got the shelf out of a building that was being demolished, and we're going to use it for some of our books. It's wonderful. We love old things, especially the things regular people had. I guess I'd like the fancy antiques, too, if I could afford them, but I can't. We save the kinds of old things most people just throw away, but with some restoration our stuff looks like something Pa and Ma and Laura and Mary might have owned.

- Caleb and Jordan played games and helped us off and on as we needed it. The computer is also in the study, so it was in use most of the day.

- Most Sunday evenings we watch a movie on TV or on the VCR. Sundays are also the day when our extended families get together. That almost always means food, playing games, and visiting with grandparents, aunts, uncles, and cousins. There are nineteen of us right here in town, and we always get together for birthdays, so we see each other often.

MONDAY:

- I usually leave for work at about 7:30 A.M., and Jordan often gets up before I leave. Caleb tends to sleep in later, but he has always required more hours of sleep than Jordan. She pretty much has the house to herself for an hour or two since Dan is usually doing chores or cutting wood for our woodstove. Jordan gets dressed and fixes herself something to eat, usually cold cereal or boiled eggs. Then she reads or just sits and thinks for a while. Caleb gets up at 10:00 or 11:00 and heads straight for the computer. When he gets hungry, he fixes himself a bowl of cereal or a salami sandwich. By this time, Dan is in the house and often starts a project to improve our house or fix something that's broken. This particular day, he brought home the runt of a set of goat kids that were just born a couple of days ago. This little guy isn't thriving the way his brother is, so we're going to hand-feed him in addition to letting him nurse from his mother. Both kids spent much of the day nurturing him.

- At 3:00 Dan dropped Caleb off at the school for basketball practice. Then he brought Jordan out to the college because she and I are sitting in on a sign language class that's being offered during the month of January. Jordan has been teaching herself to sign for a couple of years, and we both thought we could learn it faster in a class. The teacher gave us special permission to be there even though we won't be getting any credit or a grade. This first day was a little bit frustrating for both of us because the teacher finger-spells very fast, but I hope we'll get better at reading what she signs. She also told us she would finger-spell less and less as we learned more of the signs for specific words.

- This first day, Jordan was close to tears as we left the class; she felt very discouraged. We do very little direct instruction at home with the kids, but what we do is always one-on-one and directed by the needs of the individual child. This was Jordan's first experience with instruction geared for the average student or more advanced students. She decided to give it a little more time before deciding whether to remain in the class.

(continues)

- We went home at 6:00 and discovered that Caleb had already started fixing supper and was at the computer playing a strategy game. The baby goat was in a box in the kitchen, and Caleb had already bottle-fed it, so Jordan and I both just hugged the little guy for a few minutes while Caleb told us how hard basketball practice had been after two weeks off for the holidays.

- We ate quickly, because on Monday nights Caleb and Dan have Boy Scouts. Dan is an assistant leader and Caleb is a Star Scout. The scouting program is something the guys like doing together, and Jordan and I really enjoy our evening alone with each other, too. We usually play games or work on puzzles, but sometimes we watch a movie or read a book. I got her a book of Shakespeare's plays in story form, and we've been reading it together when we have a chance. The plots are so involved that she prefers reading them with me so we can stop and sort out people and events when necessary.

- This particular night we played Boggle, Skip Bo, and Probe. She won Skip Bo and Probe, and gave me a huge hug each time and told me what a great job I did. She also gave me a lesson on how to play Tetris and Mario Cart on the Super Nintendo. We laughed hysterically at my feeble attempts, and quit when my thumbs got too sore.

- When Dan and Caleb got home, we all piled onto the king-sized bed and watched part of a six-hour documentary on the Revolutionary War. We are currently part way through three other similar documentaries, one on the history of guns, one on the American West, and one on American Indians. It seems we're enmeshed in American history at the moment, but I made a mental note to find some quality movies or documentaries on Europe, too, since our family is traveling through Europe next summer for my parents' fiftieth wedding anniversary.

- At 10:00 I went to bed. I'm one of those people who needs eight to nine hours of sleep a night. Jordan decided to join me, and we finger-spelled into each others' hands in the dark until we got tired. It's thrilling, like Helen Keller and Annie Sullivan in the movies. Caleb stayed up and worked on a puzzle in the computer game The Incredible Machine. I was asleep by the time he turned off the lights and went to bed. (Dan was expecting more baby goats, and decided to sleep at the farm so he could watch for them.)

TUESDAY:

- Not much happened today. Both kids practiced piano, and Caleb helped his dad bring a load of wood to the backyard. Jordan read through her Garfield books and finished a friendship bracelet she's been working on. Caleb played on the computer, loading The Incredible Toon Machine and figuring out how all the parts worked. In the afternoon, he went to basketball and Jordan and I went to signing class.

- The evening was spent watching two shows on TV and playing games. The kids and I played Boggle while Dan worked on the radiator system in our house. We have a large woodstove outside which heats water that circulates through our house. We've installed the whole system ourselves, and are forever looking for ways to improve on its efficiency. We eventually hope to not only heat the house with it, but also heat all of our hot water, use the heat for a clothes dryer, and maybe even put in a big hot tub kind of thing. A friend of ours told us that refrigerators can even be run off such a heat source, so we have lots of research and tinkering ahead of us. Currently, we're trying to install radiators in rooms as we finish restoring them.

- Dan recently got out a radio that receives signals from all over the world. While we were playing games, Caleb kept

(continues)

jumping up to find interesting new stations for us to listen to. He was particularly thrilled with a German station, and he and his sister got a kick out of picking out German words they know. They spent the rest of the evening speaking Germish, my term for the mostly-English-with-a-German-accent language they have invented.

WEDNESDAY:

- Today Dan needed to take a friend to the hospital and neither one of the kids wanted to go along, so they came to work with me. They walked out to the college after their piano lessons, which they have every Wednesday morning. (They have always had their lessons during school hours, since after school is so busy and hectic for most piano teachers.) I took Whizzo, the baby goat, with me to the office since he would need to be fed and cared for during the day. Both kids worked on the computers, playing games, drawing pictures, and surfing the Net for most of the morning. We have a PC at home and Macs at work, so the kids are comfortable with both types. We don't have Internet access at home yet, so Caleb, especially, is always eager to look up software auctions and *Star Wars* collectibles prices. They fed themselves and the goat, and then went to the student center to play ping-pong for a while. Caleb also went to the gym to bounce his racquet ball around.

- Later, Caleb went to basketball practice and Jordan and I went to signing class. We're feeling a little bit overwhelmed by the number of signs we're learning each day, but we're getting better at reading the teacher's signs, so I guess it's paying off. I'm very glad I'm not getting credit for the class, because I tend to be very schooled and feel I have to work for the "A" in any class I'm in. Jordan, on the other hand, is working hard to keep up with the class because she wants to know sign language. She was really excited tonight because she got about half of the points on the daily quiz. We're numbering and keeping our quizzes each day so we can actually see our progress.

- On our way home from class, Jordan expressed some feelings of resentment that the class is every single day and two whole Saturdays out of the month. She wants to learn to sign, and I really think she likes the class, but she still feels the intrusion of its schedule in her life. She's used to pursuing something intensely until her interest wanes and then coming back to it at a later time. Some people would see this as a problem with unschooling, as if a student's life needs to be over-scheduled in order to get used to the real world of schedules. I maintain that spending our time on other people's schedules is yucky for many of us, even adults, and especially for the ones who have suffered from it the most. Jordan sees it as an intrusion into her life, but she's willing to suffer through it. I took the opportunity to point out how small an intrusion this particular class is compared to being in school full-time for years and years.

- During the course of the day, Whizzo's condition had deteriorated to the extent that his breathing was very labored. He died in his sleep while we were in class. Jordan had spent much of the day holding him and caring for him and was devastated that she hadn't been there for him when he needed her. We hugged and comforted each other and said good-bye to the little guy, and Dan buried him when we got home. Caleb did his best to comfort Jordan, since she takes it pretty hard when anything dies.

- Dan had supper ready, so we ate and caught up on the details of each other's lives. Wednesday nights the hockey club at the college has a family in-line skate night that we like to attend. I told the kids years ago that I would learn to skate if they would stick with piano lessons, so they're holding me to the deal. I have been enjoying the lessons. They

(continues)

hold my hand and help me up when I fall, but tonight Jordan and I decided to stay home while Dan and Caleb went skating. I spent the evening sorting through stacks of papers, trying to get organized, because the piano teacher assigned a piece for Jordan out of one of Caleb's old books that I can't find. While I was rearranging the study, Jordan drew pictures and did dot-to-dots. We talked about Whizzo several times and we signed to each other a bit, off and on.

- When Caleb got home, he was ecstatic because the hockey team let him play with them after the family skate. They made him MVP of the evening (which was very sweet of them) and invited him to join them every week. I guess Caleb had a blast. He has tried to get his friends to come to these skates, too, but since the practices are always on school nights they haven't been able to come.

- I got so caught up in listening to Caleb's stories of the evening, and showing him pictures of really fancy tree houses in a *Smithsonian* magazine, that it was 11:30 when I checked the time. I dashed off to bed and the kids and Dan followed.

THURSDAY:

- Jordan's room is pretty small and she has lots of stuff, so she spent quite a bit of time today sorting and organizing. Caleb worked on his Sim Tower for a while and then reread Tintin and Asterix books. He practiced his new piano piece, a Scott Joplin rag, but poor Jordan still has to wait for Dan or me to find her book. She played some old pieces in order to keep up her skills.

- Caleb had a basketball game today at the same time as the signing class, so Dan went to watch him alone. This was the first game I have missed, and I felt bad that I couldn't be in both places at once.

- Today in signing class, Jordan and I learned the signs for food. The teacher realized that everyone needed a break from the abstract pronouns and time words we've been working on. It was fun. I've always liked languages, and have tried to introduce the kids to German, French, and Spanish, but it just occurred to me today that learning sign language is a really good way to learn what it's like to learn other languages. Jordan's learning that things aren't always literally translated, and that learning vocabulary is time-consuming—and easier if you find some way to relate the new word to its meaning. She's also realizing that fluency will take work and time, but that it's really fun and exciting to be able to use a new language. She told me today that the class hasn't been what she expected. The teacher is pretty much just following the book and giving us time to practice with each other. She expected a class in signing to be more exciting and fun. She's decided to stick with it in order to learn signing, but I don't think she'll be asking to take any other class right away.

FRIDAY:

- The kids ran around with Dan today, shopping at thrift stores and running errands. The three of them did the grocery shopping, took care of the goats, got some money out of the bank, and did the laundry. The public school got out early today, and there was no basketball practice, so Caleb and his friends went snowboarding in the afternoon.

- After signing class, Jordan had her best friend over and the two of them did their nails and chatted in Jordan's room for hours. I helped Dan off and on with a radiator while I fixed supper. Caleb called to ask if he could go to a college basketball game with his friends, and Jordan was busy doing girl stuff, so I was left to my own devices for most of the evening. I read some magazines and visited

(continues)

with Dan. Then he and I watched a police drama on television that we wouldn't usually watch because the kids would be with us. The kids don't like to watch realistic scary stuff.

SATURDAY:

- On Saturday mornings, when we don't have to go somewhere, the kids and I watch *Pepper Ann* and *Science Court* together. We usually slice fruit for the fruit dryer while we're watching. We can get the whole dryer filled in an hour or two. Then, for the next couple of days, the house is filled with the aroma of apples, bananas, or tomatoes. We dry food when it's plentiful and then enjoy munching on it all year long.

- I like to clean, bake, and shop on Saturdays because I've learned I'm happiest when I feel like I've accomplished a lot. The children generally join me or play with each other, or—their favorite since their friends are in school all week— they call up friends and play with them all day. Rarely, we go out of town on weekends. (I don't like crowds of people in stores, so if I get the urge to go to the city to shop, we generally go during the week on a day when I don't have to work.)

- This particular Saturday, Jordan and I were in signing class for six hours. Thank goodness that doesn't happen every weekend! Caleb played basketball and a *Star Wars* card game with friends all day. Dan helped some friends move.

CHAPTER ELEVEN

Practical Considerations

UNSCHOOLING OR NOT, every homeschooling family needs to deal with certain mundane practical details in order to learn at home. If you are already homeschooling in some fashion, you are familiar with the magnitude of change it can cause in your lives. If you are just beginning, you will need to prepare yourselves to handle some new situations. The state you live in has definite rules about your child's education. Your household has financial obligations that may well become challenging to meet if one parent gives up income. Perhaps more important still, every member of your family needs to learn (or relearn) how to spend large chunks of time together.

The first step is to think seriously about why you're choosing homeschooling. Your reasons—whether they are educational, social, political, religious, or, as for most of us, some complicated combination of all of these—will affect the choices you make about how you homeschool. You'll want to think about who will be making the decisions about homeschooling; whether you're planning on a learner-centered approach like unschooling or a more structured parent-directed method, everyone in the family will have to live with those decisions. Find out how your children feel about the idea, and whether any reservations they have are due simply to unfamiliarity with the concept or if they have specific substantive concerns.

Think especially about the amount of time you will be undertaking to spend with your children. No matter how much you love your children or how convinced you are that homeschooling (or unschooling) is the best educational option for them, it will not work unless you genuinely enjoy being around your kids for large chunks of your day.

Legal Requirements

Once you are determined to undertake some form of homeschooling, you'll need to make practical decisions about how to comply with your state's laws governing compulsory school attendance. Most states require children between the ages of seven and sixteen to attend some sort of school, although the upper and lower ages vary somewhat from one state to the next.

While homeschooling is legal in one form or another in every state, not all states have statutes explicitly authorizing homeschooling. Some states consider homeschooling to be a form of private education, regulated by the same rules that govern conventional private schools. Other states regulate homeschooling directly, although the oversight varies from simple registration forms, to lengthy descriptions and reviews of curricula, to authorization by local school officials. Some states require periodic testing or other evaluation of homeschooled students; the results of such tests may determine whether the student is allowed to continue homeschooling, or may be simply for parents' information.

Whatever form your state's laws take, you'll need to find out what they are. There are several sources of such information, some more useful than others:

- Your local school district, county office of education, or state department of education.

While school officials may seem to be the most obvious, reliable source of legal information about homeschooling, this is not always the case. School officials often know little about alternatives to public schools; when this is the case, they sometimes provide information about what they think the law says, or even what they think the law ought to say, instead of what the law actually says. Where school funding is dependent on school attendance, as is most often the case in the United States, you'll sometimes get a fairly discouraging summary of the law. In some states, you may get perfectly accurate and reliable information, including offers of curriculum and other support, but it's difficult to tell unless you have some idea of the law from other sources as well.

- The applicable statutes and regulations themselves.

It's a good idea to read the applicable statutes for yourself, although this alone will not give you the complete picture. Reading the statutes will tell you what the law says and help you evaluate the advice you get from other sources, but it will not tell you much about how the law is actually enforced. It's fairly common— at least in part because of the peculiar legalese used in most statutes—for the law to sound much more onerous and demanding than is actually the case.

You can usually find your state's education code, along with other legal codes for your state, in local branch or college libraries. They are well-indexed; check under "homeschooling," "home education," "private education," "private schools," and similar terms to find the sections you need. You'll also need to check the "pocket parts" of the statute books—the updates tucked into pockets inside the back covers of the bound volumes—for any recent amendments to the statutes.

- Homeschool support groups.

Homeschool organizations are usually a good source of information about regulations. Most states have at least one, and often two or three, statewide organizations of homeschooling families. (Both *Home Education Magazine* and *Growing Without Schooling* publish lists of homeschool groups, as do several Web sites.) In those few states with no statewide groups, check for local support groups in the larger cities; they often perform some of the same functions as state groups. Such organizations usually publish guides for new homeschoolers, which, depending on the laws of that state, may be anything from a few photocopied sheets to a printed booklet to a full-fledged book. You might want to check into more than one such guide; if you find significant differences between them, you'll want to do a bit more research to find out which is more accurate. In general, though, you'll find that homeschool organizations provide solid information. They have a vested interest in getting their facts straight; if they're wrong, they're risking their own families' educational choice.

When you first look into the laws regulating homeschooling, the whole process may seem overwhelming. You may spend your first homeschooling year or two worrying that you'll mess up the paperwork requirements somehow and attract the baleful attentions of local truant officers. With a little experience, though, the worry will subside, and complying with your state's laws will become a routine matter.

To keep your worries over the legal status of homeschooling at the minimal level where they belong:

- Familiarize yourself with your state's laws regarding homeschooling.

- Join a state homeschooling organization. In addition to the basic information they provide, such groups watch for potential legal and legislative changes that could affect homeschoolers; your membership will help to support their efforts.

- Don't assume that everything you read and hear about homeschooling laws or problems is accurate. It never hurts to consider who is talking and what their motives may be.

- Don't let legal worries distract you from your homeschooling. If you find that keeping records for legal compliance is interfering with your day, you're probably keeping far more information than is necessary. Talk to other homeschoolers to see how they keep everything in perspective.

- Don't hide the fact that you homeschool. Visible homeschooling families within our communities help to make homeschooling more familiar and acceptable to the general public.

Money and Time

Homeschooling—particularly unschooling—is one of the least expensive alternatives to public school, if one considers only the cost of materials. Most unschooling families report that they acquire little in the way of books and other materials that they would not have gotten for their families anyway, and even the packaged curricula used by more structured homeschoolers rarely run as high as one thousand dollars annually per child.

But homeschooling, in whatever form, is expensive in terms of the time it demands from at least one parent. For most families, this means that one parent forgoes outside employment to stay home with the kids. Many single-income families find that financial survival is less of a hardship than they expected, and they find plenty of ways to keep expenses down without feeling that they are missing out. Most discover that they enjoy doing things together as a family, pursuing such low-cost activities as reading, gardening, making music, getting together with friends, hiking, picnicking, and so forth. It's also common for families to become less interested in the latest fads and fashions.

A great many homeschooling families end up making frugality a family challenge. They patronize yard sales and thrift shops, finding everything from books and toys to clothes and hobby equipment at bargain prices. The kids become experts at bargaining, and gain first-hand experience in determining the value of their money.

Many families, especially as their kids grow older, opt for some kind of work from home for the at-home parent. Such work varies from product sales (Discovery Toys, Dorling Kindersley Books, Usborne Books, Tupperware, Avon, etc.) to contract work in graphic art, computer programming, accounting, or Web site design, to name just a few possibilities. Home-based businesses can provide interesting learning experiences for the kids, while giving them the opportunity to perform useful work.

While the majority of homeschooling families consist of one working parent and one parent at home with the kids, there are still plenty of homeschooling families who do not fit that traditional model. Perhaps both parents are employed outside the home, but are able to stagger their schedules to care for their children. Others arrange part-time jobs for both adults and deliberately choose a lower standard of living as a fair exchange for being able to spend more time together as a family. When both parents work outside the home, considerable planning is required, but one of the real advantages of homeschooling is the flexible schedule it allows. Families can work together whenever they have the time to do so, whether it's early in the mornings or late in the evenings.

If you're a single parent, don't assume that homeschooling would be impossible for you. Single-parent homeschooling takes determination and organization, and—especially for those with young children—help. Most single parents of younger children work out flexible schedules and make child-care arrangements with other homeschooling families. Also worth looking into are cooperative learning arrangements, in which families take turns helping their children explore various topics. Another possibility is a "mother's helper"—an older neighbor child who is able to help with your kids while you get caught up on tasks at home, a teen who can take on more responsibilities such as helping with meals or other housekeeping, or, if you have the room, even a college student who can help out in exchange for room and board.

In any such case, when parents' time and energy is limited and carefully allocated, you'll find it worth the effort to cultivate a network of friends who can help at short notice when the inevitable emergencies crop up or when you find that you just plain need a break from your strenuous routine.

Siblings

What do you do when you have more than one child to homeschool? How do you give each child the individual attention she needs without ignoring the rest?

Dealing with a variety of ages can be tricky, particularly when the younger children are still toddlers or preschoolers who want to be involved with everything that's going on all the time. Older kids may have projects that need to be left undisturbed or may simply want some one-on-one time for rambling talks with a parent. Play dates and nap times can help, but patience and time are usually the only permanent solution to this particular version of the sibling problem; younger children grow up quickly and learn to handle such situations more easily.

Another version of the sibling problem is the constant squabblers. These are the kids—usually within two or three years' range in age—who pick on each other, annoy each other, and seem to derive immense satisfaction from driving each other (and their parents) crazy. Kids who begin homeschooling after a few years in school often go through a period when such battles seem much worse than when they were in school. It's only natural; because of school schedules and homework demands, they probably have not spent a great deal of time together. Suddenly homeschooling puts them in closer contact for longer stretches of time each day, and they've got to get to know each other as more than just "bratty younger sister" or "bossy older brother." With time, they'll settle down quite a bit; they may get better at irritating each other, but they'll also get better at settling their differences. Most homeschooling families find that their children eventually become much closer friends than they ever were as schoolkids.

My children are two and a half years apart. Usually I focus on one child, and the other picks up wisps and snatches from the background. It is exciting to watch the children learn exactly what they are ready for and interested in. This works wonderfully if you are willing to drop your expectations of what a particular child should be learning right now.

However, they definitely have different interests, and this seems to be more of a problem as they grow older. They become more insistent about pursuing their particular interests. For example, on a recent trip to the zoo my daughter was eager to visit all the animals, while my son couldn't be pulled away from watching the construction of a new part of the zoo. However, most of the time we coexist and learn happily together. Often the children end up learning from each other, and I from them.

We just try to be sensitive and considerate—tough lessons sometimes, but that's the kind of lesson I consider to be of prime importance.

I also try to take advantage of the times when one child is off at a friend's or at some activity. At that time, we do favorite activities together that the missing child doesn't really care for. —*Carolyn,* Pennsylvania

My girls are eight and eleven. This year our homeschool group was given the opportunity to sign up for swimming lessons and bowling classes (not a league; they actually use the bowling to teach science, math, and vocabulary). My younger wanted to do them both; my older didn't want to do either. Samantha is having a great time bowling, has shown great improvement, and has learned a lot. Ally goes with us to the bowling alley on the days when her dad has to work, but if he's home she usually stays with him. She doesn't like the noise, but I think she does enjoy watching the kids and talking with the other parents there. She also helps the moms with toddlers and infants, so this has given her an opportunity to do something she enjoys, even if it's not the main reason we are there.

Samantha also joined AWANAS, a Christian kids' club, and Ally went to one meeting, hated it, and hasn't gone back. Samantha likes the workbooks and memorization, but Ally is a perfectionist; she's self-conscious if she is not perfect the first time, and this group does not fit her personality. However, she will help her sister in reading the verses she has to memorize and drills her when asked.

The girls have some similar interests, but I think they have more differences. They do share activities, and one will help the other with things she is better at or has more interest in. Luckily, the schedules of their activities don't conflict, so each can do her own thing. Maybe if they didn't get along so well most of the time their different interests would cause strife, but they do get along and enjoy each other's company, so they each give and take in the activities they choose to do. —*Marianne*, Arizona

You'll probably find that learning with kids of different ages is not as much of a problem as you expect. With the more structured approaches to homeschooling, in which each student may work on a different subject from a different textbook than her siblings, parents can find themselves stretched to give each child the help and attention she needs. With an unschooling approach, formal preparation and direct instruction are minimal to nonexistent; parents provide help on a more relaxed, informal basis and children often work indepedently. It's also easy to tackle projects together and allow each child to work at her own level, depending on the interests and abilities of each, and unschooled kids often develop projects together, using all their skills cooperatively. You may want to check with local support groups to see what cooperative learning activities they offer; sometimes a chance to work with other kids now and then—away from the same old family members all the time—may be just what is needed.

If you worry that you won't be able to give each child enough time and attention, keep the problem in perspective: even if you can't give each of your children all the time they want with you, they're undoubtedly getting far more individual attention than they'd get in a school classroom.

Finding Moral Support

I can't emphasize enough the value of finding other homeschoolers, particularly other unschoolers, to consult with about problems and challenges. Whatever the issue, other families can help you figure out what you're dealing with—whether sibling wars are simply a stage kids go through at specific ages, whether your kids need more (or less) attention from you. Support groups can help you find community resources, keep you informed about relevant legal issues, and point you to the best thrift shops and used book stores. Chapter 12 will get you started on finding or building a support system that works for you.

Resources

Griffith, Mary. *The Homeschooling Handbook* (Prima Publishing, 1997). You'll find more detail here about dealing with legal issues, finding support groups, and coping with problem areas, along with a general overview of different approaches to homeschooling (including unschooling).

Whitehead, John W., and Alexis Irene Crow. *Home Education: Rights and Reasons* (Crossway Books, 1993). If you're looking for an in-depth discussion of the legal issues surrounding homeschooling, this is the book you want. It covers both statutes and case law, and is particularly good on constitutional issues.

CHAPTER TWELVE

Coping with Doubts and Challenges

ALL RIGHT, YOU'RE convinced. You've read about all the different unschooling families in this book, you've read about a few more in *Growing Without Schooling*, and you've even met a few unschoolers who seem to be reasonable, competent, gregarious people. You've talked the whole concept of unschooling over with your family; your spouse likes the idea and your kids are eager to get started. You just know that once you begin unschooling, your kids will quit watching so much television, bicker less with each other and with you, and beg for twice-weekly trips to the library. Once you start unschooling, life will go much more smoothly, and you'll no longer need to worry about how your kids will turn out.

Maybe you'll win the lottery, too.

Your kids may well watch less television and read more on their own than they would if they were in school. You'll all probably find you have more time to allocate to things you want to do. It's even fairly likely that, after a short period of adjustment, you and your kids will get along better than when they were in school. But even unschooling will not change the fact that you are parents, and one of the unavoidable aspects of being parents is worrying about your kids.

You'll suffer from niggling little worries and nagging doubts: your daughter is reading too many Babysitters Club and Goosebumps books and not enough worthwhile literature; your son doesn't quite grasp the decimal number system, and you doubt that he'll ever find a reason to buckle down and learn it. But you'll manage to function pretty well with a constant low level of fretting, only occasionally nagging your kids to accomplish at least one constructive thing each day.

> Even unschooling will not change the fact that you are parents, and one of the unavoidable aspects of being parents is worrying about your kids.

Thus far, I haven't had any panic attacks. I wonder if I'm doing enough at times or if the kids are missing some vital subject, but it's pretty low-key. Having done lots of reading and been intimately involved with alternative education for six years, I'm pretty secure in my beliefs. I see us doing some fine-tuning, perhaps, but nothing drastic. It would be nice to find more local support, but I'm not holding my breath.
—*Ruth,* Montana

But one day your sister-in-law starts raving about the wonderful new program at her kids' school that has them performing adaptations of fairy tales for the kindergartners and first-graders—in Spanish, no less. Suddenly that low level of vexation blooms into a full-blown PPA—the dreaded Parental Panic Attack!

Parental Panic Attacks (the term is flippant, but the feelings it describes are seldom amusing) can be prompted by comments or criticisms from neighbors, friends, or (especially) relatives, or by the unflattering comparisons we make between ourselves and other unschooling families. Whatever prompts them, though, it's important to keep PPAs in perspective; don't make any sudden changes in your educational approach. Overreacting can have deleterious effects on both your family and your bank account.

> My parental panic attacks usually result in the purchase of more books or other resources, which I often end up selling since they don't meet our needs. —*Cathy R.,* Pennsylvania

> My kids have learned to handle my panic attacks fairly well. I always think I'm being very low-key in suggesting that they might want to work on whatever it is that's bothering me this time. Mostly they laugh—"Mom's on one of her crusades again!"—and then they do something completely un-related to impress me, after which I slink off and leave them again to their capable selves. —*Ann,* California

Take some time to figure out whether your worry is simply the sort of generalized worry that all parents subject themselves to from time to time. After all, if your kids were in school, you'd be worried, too, but about things like peer pressure, class size, grades, standard-ized tests, teacher qualifications, textbook quality, and so on. Take a good look at your kids, too—at what they're like and how they spend their time. You may realize that your fears are more about some hy-pothetical future possibility than about something concrete in the here-and-now.

Sometimes what you need is just a bit of outside help—activities for yourself or your kids outside the home, or access to other people who can help your kids explore interests to greater depth than you're interested in or able to.

> How much outside help you need depends on you and your children. In areas I'm not particularly interested in or knowledgeable about, I seek outside help. For my daughter, who learns best in social situations and is interested in people, we put ourselves in social situations. My son, on the other hand, is able to keep himself intellectually active all by himself and people can be a distraction, so he stays home more often. However, I do try to find outside opportunities for him, too, because I believe that the

outside world is a wonderful place for an education. This is one of the great advantages of homeschooling—being able to observe the real world in action and being able to find people passionate about their activities who will share them with the children. Finding these people is a very important part of my job, and will become even more important as the children get older. —*Carolyn,* Pennsylvania

Talking with other people about your needs and concerns can be extremely helpful when you're trying to decide whether your worries are just normal parental hysteria or they actually have a legitimate basis. You may find, however, that those who look askance at your unschooling may not be terribly sympathetic to your concerns, even though they may view their own school-related concerns in an entirely different light.

We all have had panic attacks. I find that if I am really overcome with worry, I try to trace the worry to its source, which tends to be worry about the economy, the environment, our financial security, health insurance. Rarely is it really about the way we live; it's more about the trying world in which we live and how to make it a sensible place. When my kids have worries about their "abilities," they usually come to me and tell me, and we then talk about ways to rectify the situation. Worries are frequently like weather conditions; they pass.

I have been extremely insecure at times and also very lonely. I have some good friends, but none of them approves of homeschooling (let alone unschooling) enough to ever discuss it. I don't dare express doubts about it or I'd just be proving them right. Of course, they talk to me often of their own dissatisfaction with their kids' teachers, homework, schoolmates, etc. —*Susan,* Iowa

As far as my panic attacks go, I have always sought encouragement and support from my friends.

Also, *Growing Without Schooling* has greatly validated our adventure. In fact, so have some public school teachers along the way, including the kids' second-grade teacher, who initially encouraged me to homeschool. The kids don't seem to have any panic attacks, having already been in school, having begged to be homeschooled. The thing they express is a desire to go to a prom, and they wonder how that will happen if they aren't in high school. —*Liane,* California

If you're lucky, you'll have good friends or relatives who are willing to talk with you about your doubts and worries, who will support you while you try to work out solutions. But no matter how helpful such friends are, there will be times when you'll want to talk to other unschoolers, to people who understand what you're going through because they've been through it themselves. At such times, a good homeschool support group is worth seeking out.

Q: Do you worry sometimes about keeping up with other kids?

SHAUNA (13): I think trying to keep up with other people is not worth it. What does their learning speed have to do with yours? I don't worry about trying to keep up with other kids my age, because as long as I'm learning at *my* speed, what's to worry about? Getting into college or starting a job is almost always uncertain. There are things I'll worry about when the time comes. For now, I'm just learning what I want to learn at my speed. Set curriculums are *not* my thing!

Organized Support Groups

The trick in finding a good support group for yourself is knowing what you're looking for. Support groups come in all varieties and sizes, and the first one you find may not offer what you want. Groups range from small, informal gatherings of just a few families to highly structured organizations with several hundred members. In urban and suburban areas, you may find several existing groups to choose from; in less populated areas, you may be lucky to find any organized group at all.

What kind of support can homeschool groups provide? Most offer informal get-togethers such as park days and skate days—regular scheduled opportunities just to meet and spend time with other homeschooling families—and most publish at least a minimal newsletter with information about scheduled events and activities. Larger or more active groups may also schedule field trips to museums, businesses, historical parks, or other sites that interest their members. Some also organize cooperative learning activities, such as writing or science clubs, choirs or theatrical groups, sports teams, and so forth.

> The trick in finding a good support group for yourself is knowing what you're looking for.

Every group has its own style and personality, so you shouldn't expect that you will be happy or comfortable with every group you contact. Some groups are organized around characteristics such as unschooling or particular religious beliefs, but it's not uncommon for such specialization to exist on an informal or unannounced basis. In such cases, it may take you a few weeks or months to learn enough about a group to determine whether it's really what you're looking for; don't feel obligated to stick with a group that doesn't meet your needs.

Unschoolers, especially, sometimes have trouble finding groups of like-minded families. Particularly in the larger organizations, there can be a kind of homeschooling-parent peer pressure to adopt particular curricula or textbooks or hold rigid views about children and learning. (Unschooling groups, of course, are sometimes just as rigid in their customs and beliefs.) If you happen to agree with those views, you probably won't have much of a problem. But if your views differ, you may find yourself fending off those panic attacks you were seeking help to avoid.

If existing groups in your area don't have much to offer, you may want to try starting your own. You can post notices on bulletin boards in local libraries, community centers, food co-ops, churches, and other places likely to attract the sort of families you seek. You may also be able to advertise in newsletters of fairly structured support groups for other unschoolers; often such groups have quite a few unschooling members who would be happy to find others to share ideas and experience with.

When I started homeschooling Amie, we were very alone. The other homeschoolers we knew about all lived at least an hour away from us, and there were very few Amie's age. We started a homeschoolers' support group that met in our home for several years. This still didn't help build a group of homeschooling friends for Amie, as this idea was so new that most of those attending were parents of children under school age who were wondering if this was for them. When the homeschooling movement began to grow, the groups near us were mostly fundamentalist Christian, and their approach to homeschooling was very structured and very different from ours.

When Tessa was four, a friend and I started our "play group," which consisted of about six families. We met in rotating homes once a week, and whoever hosted that week would plan the activity. This meant a wonderful variety of activities: trips to Science World, fantastic crafts, hikes in the woods, imaginative learning games, science experiments. We continued our play group for several years, until some of the children went to school and some moved away. We still miss this group sorely. This provided me with the best support group, and the children with a wonderful group of friends who were doing the same things they were doing. I think this made it easier to get past the starting-school age, when many children wonder if they're missing something when they see the other kids on the block heading off to school.

The Vancouver homeschool group is much more suited to our style, but is a long drive away. I have recently attended one of their meetings (after meaning to do so for almost a decade!), and I think it will be worth the drive to go now and then. They also have a wonderful assortment of field trips and activities that go on year-round.

We have tapped into many field trips and activities that happen with homeschoolers in our area, too. Last month we went to a science and engineering workshop hosted by our local homeschool group. Three University of British Columbia engineering students came out and put on the workshop. It was quite instructive and entertaining. It's funny to think of field trips when we're so constantly on the go! If we were to label our outings as field trips, we sure have lots of them! —*Terry*, British Columbia

Other Support Options

Sometimes, of course, there just aren't enough unschoolers around to make an organized group work. But there are plenty of other routes to finding support for unschooling.

First are homeschooling periodicals. *Growing Without Schooling (GWS)* and *Home Education Magazine (HEM)* are the longest established and best known of those that appeal to unschoolers. *GWS* is more focused toward unschooling; *HEM* is also supportive of unschooling, but does not focus on it exclusively. The contents of both are largely written by homeschooling parents, although *GWS* especially has begun to publish more pieces by teens and "grown-up" unschoolers.

There are also other, smaller publications that specifically target unschoolers. *F.U.N. News* focuses on a single topic—such as geography, foreign languages, or socialization—in each quarterly issue, along with regular columns, information on interesting Web sites, and comparative reviews of books, software, and other materials. *Family Learning Exchange* covers unschooling and natural learning, with reader-written reviews and opinion pieces.

Perhaps most useful to unschoolers looking for ongoing support and advice are the Internet mailing lists. Like printed unschooling resources, they contain plenty of useful information, but they also have the great advantage of being interactive. That interactivity can be a mixed blessing, however; it means that the message volume on the lists is usually high, and there is lots of off-topic banter and debate. If you're looking to find specific information quickly, the mailing lists are an iffy proposition; you may get a dozen answers to your question within a few hours, your question may be buried in the latest debate over the merits of television or breast-feeding, or you might be ignored entirely.

When joining mailing lists, it's usually a good idea to lurk for a while—perhaps a week or two—to learn something of the customs of the list and the styles of the regulars before you post much. If nothing else, it can save you from a good roasting when you respond in outraged seriousness to a post that was written with tongue firmly in cheek.

If what you seek is a rowdy and rambling discussion of all sorts of ideas about learning, liberally sprinkled with humor, unsolicited advice, stories of unschooling successes and failures, and the occasional raucous flame-fest, the lively communities of unschoolers online may be for you.

I'm an avid reader of the Unschooling List, and occasionally lurk on AOL's Home Education Magazine and Homeschooling boards, as well as CompuServe's Homeschool Alt/Ed section. I enjoy these because they seem to offer all sorts of advice in a medium I'm comfortable with accepting or tossing, as I see fit. —Jo, Louisiana

Despite having homeschooled in three states, we have never belonged to a support group. We have, on rare occasions, done things with an existing group as visitors. We have used a few outside lessons (swimming, art, and, currently, fencing). We've generally done our own field trips. My support early on came from *HEM*, *GWS*, homeschooling books, and the few homeschoolers I knew well enough to call occasionally. In later years, I also joined a couple of homeschooling round-robins and I acquired pen pals, and now, of course, I have the Unschooling List. Generally, all I need to do is think about the alternative and I know it's a phase we're going through; homeschooling at its worst is better than institutional school. I think the kids wish that at least once they'd had a homeschooling group for finding friends. We've never had many kids in the neighborhood. —*Carol,* Florida

I only know one other unschooler in the area. I belong to the local support network to find out about field trips and find friends for the kids, rather than as a source of support for me. Most of the group is "school in a box" and assigned-work-type homeschoolers. The unschoolers and other people on AOL are who I go to for support. Many of them are in the same situation: no local unschoolers.

I have found support on the Unschooling List. My relief was so profound I was shocked at it—shocked to realize how insecure and lonely I was before I found the list. Now I know how important it is for me to be with and hear from other people like myself, even if it's only through e-mail.

It's also made me think of how wonderful it would be for my kids if they knew other unschoolers, especially Jordan, who often experiences doubts about herself and unschooling. Right now I only have e-mail at work, so the kids aren't online, but we're getting hooked up in the next week or two. How nice it would be if they found other homeschoolers to write to. Or maybe we could even find a group within a couple of hours of us to visit. That would be heaven. —*Susan,* Iowa

Special Circumstances

For some families, special circumstances—special needs, learning differences, single-parent unschooling, religious beliefs, and the like—

Q: What sorts of comments do you hear about your unschooling?

SHAUNA (13): I've been questioned about homeschooling lots of times, mostly by kids in my church youth group. The most often-asked questions are:

- I bet you get to sleep in and go to school in your pajamas, right?

- Don't you miss your friends?

- You homeschool? What's two times two?

- Do you take a test every year to see if you're keeping up?

Questions like these remind me how ignorant many people are about the many wonderful things about homeschooling, besides the fact that I get to sleep in!

make that normal, everyday, low-level worrying more difficult to cope with. Not only do they have to deal with the routine ups and downs that unschooling always entails, but they have their own specialized concerns to handle. Consider the experience of one mother of a special-needs unschooler:

I have some special comments I want to make about Parental Panic Attacks. Our second child, our son (now nearly fourteen), is a special case. He weighed less than two pounds when he was born and so was labeled "special needs" from the beginning. In some ways, that has made it more difficult to unschool him, although I am more and more finding that it is probably even *more* important to unschool him than to unschool our daughter. Or maybe the correct description is that it is even more important to unschool myself about him.

When we had so many different professionals following him for such a long time, all telling us how he was behind in this or that area, it became ever more difficult not to think that all kinds of professional intervention was needed to ensure that he didn't lag even farther behind, to help him "catch up." And from the time he was three-and-a-half until he was eight, we did just that, although for two of those years we had started our adventure of homeschooling. Most of what I remember of those years was taking him to therapy appointments three mornings a week. While that gave me uninterrupted time with his sister while he was with the therapists, I don't remember either of us (my son or me) having much time or energy or interest to do much else "academic" during those years.

Then we moved, and therapy was no longer available. What that has allowed us to do in the last six years is to realize that our son doesn't need to be "fixed," but only to be allowed to develop on his own timetable and in his own way. Yes, some modifications will probably have to be made for him for the rest of his life—he will never have the speed of judgment necessary to drive a car, for example—but he can and will do whatever he wants or needs to do when he is ready. These years have demystified the role of professionals, as well. I have come to discover that most of what they do is just common sense, and I have a healthy dose of that myself! We are fortunate that, despite many areas of special challenge, he is very bright. Knowing that the school system would have obsessed on his lack of the so-called basic skills and not fed his mind and spirit has helped the PPAs (and my mother's concerns!).

It has taken me years to be sure that unschooling works even with children like him, but I am utterly and totally convinced now that it does and is the gentlest, most respectful, most healing approach to use. He has chosen to work on some areas that are very difficult for him, doing things I never would have dreamed possible and would not have attempted to "teach" if I had been so inclined. I cannot honestly say that his self-esteem is totally intact—he had eighteen months of public schooling and is, after all, a teenager now—but I know it is in far better shape than it would have been if he had spent more years in school. As for how a parent deals with home-schooling a child with this level of need, I honestly think that unschooling rather than more structured homeschooling gives you the distance, if you will, to allow the child to own his performance and not feel guilty about all the things he can't do. Yes, there are days (weeks? months?) when I wonder if I've done all I could or should to help him maximize his potential, but then I remember it's his education, not mine, and he is doing what he needs to—and I can relax, at least a little. —*Anonymous*

Fortunately, there are publications, Web sites, and mailing lists for almost every category of specialized interest. With a little digging—the Home Ed and Unschooling Lists are good places to start—you're almost guaranteed to find resources that address your particular needs. (And if you don't, you can always start something of your own—after all, there are undoubtedly other unschoolers out there looking for the same solutions you are!)

Resources

Periodicals

At Our Own Pace: A Newsletter for Homeschooling Families with Special Needs, Jean Kulczuk, 102 Willow Drive, Waukegan, IL 60087.

Family Learning Exchange produces *FLExOnline,* a free e-mail newsletter on natural learning, family learning, and homeschooling. Contact FmlyLrngEx@ AOL.com for information.

Growing Without Schooling, 2269 Massachusetts Avenue, Cambridge, MA 02140; 617-864-3100; www.holtgws.com.

Home Education Magazine, P.O. Box 1587, Palmer, AK 99645; 907-746-1336; HEM-info@home-ed-magazine.com; www.home-ed-magazine.com.

Online Lists

Home Ed List (to subscribe, send message "subscribe" to home-ed-request @world.std.com). Home Ed is one of the oldest and largest homeschooling mailing lists. While not exclusively devoted to unschooling, there are a substantial number of unschoolers who post regularly and articulately. Home Ed also has two digest versions available.

Radical Unschoolers List (to subscribe, send message "subscribe ru" to majordomo@serv1.ncte.org). Rad Un is one of the newer unschooling lists, formed for those who wanted to avoid the occasional discussions of Saxon math or phonics programs to be found on the Unschooling List.

Unschooling List (to subscribe, send message "subscribe unschooling-list" to majordomo@ctel.net). The Unschooling List is an extremely active list with about seven hundred subscribers. It's a very friendly and easygoing list, although members do not take kindly to being told there are too many off-topic posts; their philosophy is that if unschooling is life, then everything is fair game for discussion. (The Unschooling List is also an excellent place to ask about specialized newsletters and mailing lists, since several subscribers regularly track such resources.)

CHAPTER THIRTEEN

Is Unschooling Contagious?

W E HOMESCHOOLERS ARE a pretty diffident bunch of folks. We're happy enough to tell you about unschooling if you ask us, but we wouldn't dream of pushing our educational approach on you. "This is what works for us," we say. "You might find some of these ideas useful for your family, but not everyone is cut out to be an unschooler."

This reluctance to evangelize unschooling has a number of causes. Part of it is sensitivity to conventional skepticism or even hostility toward homeschooling in general; if the general public doesn't approve of parents teaching their own children at home using conventional methods, what are they likely to think of unschooling? Partly it's simple courtesy; we don't want to imply criticism of your own educational choices by bragging about our own. Partly, though, our reserve is simply false modesty.

Scratch the surface a bit, probe a little more into our ideas and beliefs about how our kids learn, and you're likely to get a lengthy discourse on the reasons for and the advantages of unschooling for *any* child. Beneath the surface of that unpretentious practitioner of a somewhat unconventional educational alternative, you're likely to find a fierce advocate for unschooling.

In the introduction to this book, I mentioned that unschoolers, like any other variety of homeschooler, love to talk about what they do and why they do it—and that the unschooling parents who completed my questionnaire for this book were no exception. Most wrote me several pages about how their kids learned to read and otherwise feed their fascination with the world around them. But two questions elicited a far greater response than any of the others. One was, logically enough, the first: "What does the term 'unschooling' mean to you?" Based on all the conversations I've had with other unschoolers over the past decade, I expected fairly lengthy responses to that one (and you read a good portion of them in the first chapter).

But the avalanche of answers I got in response to the other question took me completely by surprise. I asked "How has unschooling affected your life as a whole? Has it affected you or your kids more? What effects do you think unschooling will have on the adults your kids become? How will they be different from more conventionally educated people?" (There was also another part to this question; we'll get to that a bit later.) It seems that the effects of unschooling on kids, on parents, and on families go far beyond what anyone expected when they first began to consider what they thought was just a simple little educational idea.

For me, unschooling has meant a very different relationship with Andrea. I no longer find myself having to find ways to coerce her into doing what I think she should be doing academically. Instead, I look for the learning that happens on its own, and marvel at how well it happens. I worried that she would not make use of her talents if I didn't "do something." Being a teacher was something that came naturally to me, so having a daughter who didn't really want to be taught has taken some adjustment. Now I feel more like a resource, and I do more suggesting than anything else.

I've also come to see how much of the school stuff is really just busy-work, with a lot of effort put into substantiating the learning. For years, I'd known that my success in school had more to do with my ability to play the game of school very well, memorizing easily for tests without any effort to really learn the material. In many ways, watching Andrea actually learn for her-self, without all the external carrots and sticks, has been a confirmation of my feelings about my own education.

For Andrea, unschooling has meant that she could concentrate on the things she enjoys without interruption. She has always been good at keeping herself busy, and my early efforts to "teach" her were, more often than not, seen as an infringement on her freedom. Now when we do take a few min-utes to try something "schoolish" (and this doesn't happen often!), it's more of a novelty. When she's had enough, we stop.

> It seems that the effects of unschooling on kids, on parents, and on families go far beyond what anyone expected when they first began to consider what they thought was just a simple little edu-cational idea.

It has also meant that she can be herself without being labeled in one way or another by the school system. She is so unbe-lievably "normal" now, although there are still scars from her battles at school. I hope that because I'm learning to give her enough freedom to learn in her own way, she will grow up feeling good about who she is. She already has a very clear sense of that, and I suspect will be as full of right-eous indignation about whatever she chooses to fight for as an adult as she is now. I think the whole concept of learning for your own reasons is ap-plicable to all of life. People usually find out at some point that it's easier to learn when it's something you want to do, but growing up in this environ-ment should produce people with a genuine love of learning.

I think that we, as unschoolers, learn to trust our children, and that is also an important concept. By and large, society tends to underestimate kids, and by giving them the freedom to explore possibilities, we have an opportunity to demonstrate how much more many kids could be doing. My big gripe with our local school was that they didn't value Andrea's strengths, which—from my perspective—were strengths that a learning institution should have valued. I always wonder how many other bright children are being crammed into those round holes, and remind myself that Andrea wouldn't let herself be. —*Stefani,* New Hampshire

Boy, has unschooling affected my life! It's a whole new way of looking at life, appreciating things, finding and recognizing and *acknowledging* one's natural interest in things. It's appreciation of children—who they are and where they are in their growth journeys. I'd love to think that this time together will make them more sensitive, fair, and caring adults, but they're also so young that many different factors could affect that between now and then. They are, however, sensitive, fair, and caring children, which makes at least our little part of the world that much more enjoyable. —*Jo,* Louisiana

I've always said that homeschooling in any form is really a lifestyle choice and not just an educational choice. Unschooling just makes it more so. It is a decision to put children first, to respect their needs and opinions, to treat them as fully human beings and not as property. I find that unschooling has allowed me to live more the way that I want to live, in a slower, more deliberate, more thought-out way, and not in the rat race of constant busyness and rushing from one thing to another. I lived in that way before we began homeschooling, and I am currently trying to figure out ways never to return to it even when the kids are grown. Unschooling has made my life fuller and richer, allowed me the "excuse" to learn things for myself, helped me to learn many things from my children. —*Carol,* Florida

Unschooling has become my life. There is nothing in my life that cannot be linked to unschooling in some way or another. I plan to always call myself an unschooler, because I will never stop learning. But I really do not think about it all that much; it's just what we do, like eating and breathing and sleeping. I am very thankful for the time it has given me to explore and learn about myself and who I am, and the freedom it has given me to ask all those burning questions and not be considered an idiot or weird. Or worry about what my hair looks like today, whether my clothes are in fad, or whether my teacher will be in a really bad mood today.

I have been able to grow faster and in more alternative ways because I am not constantly bombarded by people telling me what to do. I have a much better relationship with my brother and mother because I live with them *all* the time, so we *have* to work the problems out. I can deal with people of all ages much more easily than some of my schooled peers, because I have been able to spend more time with them. I am much slower in my pace of life. I do not have to be constantly busy, going to this activity or that one. I know how to deal with boredom and fear, and how to sit just for the pure sake of sitting and not doing anything at all.

Many people think I am much older than I am, and I think that is partly due to unschooling, in that I know more than most kids my age about a variety of subjects. But I am also willing to learn, and say "I don't know" and "Could you help me?" and "Do you know how to do this another way?" and take correction—because I know they are not out to get me, and even if they are I can still learn from their opinion.

Unschoolers are a different breed from those who have had a more conventional education and way of life. There is this aura of freedom that surrounds us, and most people are very jealous of it. We are confident and self-assured even when we are nervous. We have a much better handle on who we are and who we want to become than most people have. Even if we don't know what we want to do when we have to work, we probably know some things we *don't* want to do. *—Chase*, Florida

Unschooling has deeply affected our lives in general. My attitudes toward society have changed—or, I should say, have become more clear. When we took that first anxiety-filled step away from public school, I realized that we were leaving behind our place in society as well—casting off a whole life. I knew that people would view us differently, maybe antagonistically; I knew that I was now standing up for my beliefs by living them where people could see and pass judgment. It has led to being more forthright in all aspects of my life, and to having more courage in confrontations of all sorts. It's easier to see the charades of society, and how so much importance is connected to being part of a herd. The herd mentality is obvious in what's popular, how stupid it all seems. I am unsure how not going to school has changed the children, except I do know that they aren't much interested in most of their so-called peers and the trappings that go along with the social mores of that age group. I don't know, ultimately, if they'll be any different from most conventionally educated people, but I surely hope so. —*Liane,* California

We adults have learned so much. We have learned academically because of the answers we search out with the children. We have learned about other people because our relationships with the family have taken on added importance and because there are many relationships between the children and others outside our family. We have seen firsthand that people learn and develop differently, and so we have learned tolerance toward others. We have learned that children are often mirrors of ourselves. When we're confused, they are, too; when we're peaceful, they are, too; when we're frightened, they are, too. We have learned more about ourselves and our relationship to God. This job requires faith in something beyond ourselves and the ability to explain that faith to eager-to-learn children. It has caused us to think more about education and what it truly means.

It has created more of a team atmosphere in the family, instead of the traditional hierarchical structure. We each contribute to the team what we can. We have our traditional roles, including contributing structure to the children's lives, but additionally, the children contribute by designing and implementing their own education. It has given the children more of a sense of worth than those who submit to another educational authority. I'm hoping that this team atmosphere may avoid some grief when the children reach their teen years. —*Carolyn,* Pennsylvania

Unschooling has confirmed for me what I have suspected since high school: children are capable, willing, and able to learn whatever they choose to learn. Learning is fun, energizing, and challenging, and it takes responsibility. If you take the responsibility away from children, they have no stake in the outcome (their livelihood, family, and happiness), and instead learn how to follow orders above solving problems. I believe that patience is the biggest change for me. I need to practice it more now that I know how valuable it is. —*Emilie,* Washington

Unschooling has affected my whole life. It's hard to say whether it's affected us or our son more, since we're all in it together. I had the experience of being the parent of a child in school, and it controlled so much of our lives: bedtime, lunches, getting up, working out homework versus family time together, when or whether we traveled. And, worst of all, it put us in constant conflict with people who thought they had the right to dictate how our child should be raised. When we were in a school's home-study program, we had to account to the state in a way that made no sense to us. The feeling of freedom when we threw off that yoke was incredible. People who have yet to break loose cannot know what it is like. This is almost like a different dimension. Life is bigger and freer. People who are tied to schools for "home schooling" cannot know how different it is when you're out on your own. I feel that unschooling families often know a lot more about the nature of learning and education than just about anybody. It's unfortunate that professional educators are generally not able to grasp that. We have a lot we could teach them, and I'm still always surprised when I realize that they think it's the other way around.

As time goes by, I'm more and more stunned by the questions people ask: "What gave you the idea you were capable of teaching your child in the first place?" The question seems strange enough, but they picture me sitting and "teaching" him as if he's an empty vessel who can't learn on his own. What an obnoxious image that brings to my mind, and yet it's a perfectly natural thing for people to think. "How do you know what he's supposed to be learning?" Huh? In a world as vast and complex as this one, how did we ever come to this mutual understanding that there is just one

neat package of stuff one needs to get into one's head to be "educated."
Who is the official authority on what he's "supposed to be learning"?
"What are you going to do about high school?" This one is always said with
a funny tone of voice I have yet to quite get. Are they referring to the prom
thing? Or cliques? Having a locker? Or are they worried about biology or
algebra being mysterious things that can only be learned by sitting in a row
of desks while listening to someone "teach"? Or is it the concern that some
have expressed aloud that he won't know how to deal with bullies if he
doesn't have to bounce off them in school? What is this thing called "high
school" that concerns people so much?—*Lillian,* California

Unschooling is tied up with a lot of other lifestyle choices. It fits our
whole parenting philosophy of giving kids choices whenever possible and
respecting them as people. Unschooling has changed our lives for the better. We now have an educational method that matches our parenting
style. We were constantly fretting over problems we saw at the kids' school.
Now that worry is gone. Also gone is the hassle of getting up in the morning,
rushing through breakfast, and gathering lunches, books, and other stuff.
Gone is the need to tether our life so closely to someone else's clock. If
Sarah wants to read for four hours, she can.

I also have changed, in that I trust my kids more. The past year has
shown me that without pressure or force, they will learn, and often learn
more than if I were in control. I see myself as a facilitator and guide. It also
has caused me to question other things in our society that are long-held
"truths." I've disproved the one that says "kids won't learn without being
forced"; what else is false?

The kids haven't so much changed as they have relaxed and gotten
in tune with themselves again. Their time in school was supposed to have
been child-led, and so they always had more control and freedom than in
most educational settings. They have adjusted quite well to taking responsibility for their learning. They are usually confident that if they really want to
do something or learn about it, they have the skills and abilities to do it.
They don't wait for an adult to tell them what needs to be done. They also
do things to their own standards, not an external guide. I am asked for my

opinion on projects or other things, but as an equal or someone with a bit more experience, not as a judge or giver of grades. —*Ruth*, Montana

Changing my perspective in the educational realm has changed it in so many other areas. I am a significantly different person because of this shift. I value my children as individuals more now than when I viewed them as charges I was responsible for. We are free to form more personal relationships. Giving folks freedom to look at things their own way and go about tasks differently than I would has affected the way I interact with people I meet on a day-to-day basis. The kids are regaining some of the natural curiosity they were blessed with as toddlers, and are beginning to try to determine what it is they want to do with a day instead of just moving through it without thinking about it. Still, though, I think I've benefited more as I relax and enjoy learning with my children. If nothing else, I've rekindled the joy of learning in myself—even in areas I didn't know I enjoyed, like science. I hope that the kids will grow up knowing their own minds. —*Cathy R.*, Pennsylvania

It's made us—or at least me—more open to listening to apparently radical positions (not necessarily in a political sense) that people have on various other things. So far, I think it's affected us more. But I expect that, in time, it will affect the kids more since they'll be deprived of the experience of being incarcerated and institutionalized at an early age, forced to hew to the whims of often-idiotic adults, and required to stop learning in order to pay attention to what someone else thinks is currently important, like taking attendance or talking about administrivia.

What I see in my kids, and in other kids being home-schooled, and perhaps even more in those unschooled, is a great interest in learning—a real fire to learn—the very thing that seems to die (or be killed off) in school. I also see them retain a great sense of freedom and self-respect. They feel able to interact with people of all ages, and relatively devoid of the sense that talking to a younger kid or doing something with him or her is somehow demeaning. Less peer-

pressured, more self-assured, more considerate, and very much independent and willing to think for themselves.

I think that they're going to see themselves as able to do what they want, within the reasonable constraints of being part of a civil society. And I see them as not being part of the herd, trained to follow orders and instructions without making trouble—perhaps not very good factory workers, but probably good leaders and independent business people.
—*Patrick,* California

Unschooling has affected our life drastically. I worked full-time since my kids were six weeks old and missed most of their babyhood. I now get to be home and make up a little for all that lost time. That is the upside. The downside is that it has caused our income to be cut in half. I was making about $30,000 a year plus a free three-bedroom townhouse and free utilities as a property manager in the San Francisco Bay Area. We now live in southern California (cheaper cost of living) and pay rent on a two-bedroom apartment; the kids have to share a room. We clip coupons, cook mainly from scratch, and watch our bills daily. We are looking at other ways to either bring in more money or cut down on money spent, but I don't know how much more we can change. Unschooling is more work than a canned curriculum; it forces you to be more creative, open-minded, experimental, and patient. It also requires trusting that your children will learn and will succeed in their "studies" on their own.

My children are much happier now that we are using a more relaxed approach. They learn more and retain more than they ever did before. They are happier to learn and more eager to explore now that they know they aren't being pushed or forced.

I think my children will be different from more conventionally educated people in that they will not lose their love of learning as most children do in school. I recently read a book that said most adults have a syndrome that is like a "hardening of the brain"—kind of a stoppage of learning. It said that most adults become resistant to learning after a while because they lost the love for it as children. I don't think that will happen to children who are encouraged to explore and investigate their world on their own as they need it. I think learning will remain as natural to them as eating or breathing.

Unschooling would be helpful to all children: It's not one particular way of learning; it's learning at your own level, in your own interest, and at your own pace. What child wouldn't benefit from a learning experience like that? —*Laura Y.,* California

I hope with all my soul that my children will be different from conventionally educated people. I hope that they will know freedom rather than bondage; creativity rather than conformity; courage rather than blind obedience; intelligence rather than rote learning. I believe that conventional schools damage—perhaps irrevocably—the ability to explore, discover, and imagine. I believe that schools force us to set aside the ability to think for ourselves, to be motivated by joy and interest, to be open and honest. We hope to reap values of intelligence, honesty, caring, and self-confidence. Quite frankly, I'm not sure most of the world will ever be ready for unschooling. Too many are unable to escape the effects of conventional schooling and culture; they can no longer think for themselves or see any alternatives to the way things are. —*Amy,* Idaho

> Unschooling would be helpful to all children: It's not one particular way of learning; it's learning at your own level, in your own interest, and at your own pace. What child wouldn't benefit from a learning experience like that?

Sometimes it's difficult to determine if we are unschoolers because of our differences or different because we are unschoolers. We have a more questioning attitude toward our society and culture. For example, what are the implications of funeral ceremonies? why do people do those things? what would happen if we didn't have funerals? etc. etc. Sometimes it seems as if it would be simpler if we didn't question accepted practices so often. Yet a fuller understanding of why funerals exist has increased our appreciation of them. And because, as adults, we question, our children question as well. We, the parents, are called on to explain why we live the sort of life we do. This means we are regularly called on to understand and defend our deeply held beliefs and to incorporate them into our daily lives in a conscious way.

I have become ever more aware of the value of quietness: how loudly example speaks, how thoroughly story communicates ideas and concepts better than direct teaching, how really capable we all are. Just before the Gulf War, a series of reports was released on our national weakness in geography knowledge. Once the war began, all sources of maps containing details of Kuwait and the Gulf sold out no matter how often they were reprinted. When people felt a need to know something about a geographic area, they sought it out, even paying money so they could learn about and understand what was important to them.

Unschooling also shows what depth, not breadth, can do. So many of the people we admire as heroes in our society (even those sports stars) make their passion their work. They have a narrow focus and shut out all those things that do not relate. I think we need generalists, too, but the emphasis on "well-roundedness" in our culture ignores the fact that there are other ways to live a fulfilling life. —*Cindy,* Wisconsin

Since grade-school, I have been a "good" student. By that I mean that I played the games—happily—and jumped through the hoops in order to get the prizes. My own sense of self-worth has always been tightly connected to my schooling experience. I really have to watch myself and bite my tongue often in order to refrain from using school motivators with my kids. They both are very much motivated by intrinsic rewards when they learn about something. They don't pursue anything unless they want to for some reason of their own. I think this is great, but sometimes I catch myself luring them toward learning something for the "wrong" reasons, the reasons I always learned things: to be the best, to impress someone, to make more money, and so on. Unschooling has shown me how flimsy these reasons really are. I have had a total of twenty-four years of schooling. I guess I shouldn't be surprised that it has had such an effect on me. I am pleased, though, to see myself in my graduate courses caring more for the learning and (a little) less for the grades. I'm glad my kids won't have so much to unlearn.

My kids will be wonderful adults. They will make decisions and know that they are affected by those decisions. I can't see them whining about how much they hate their jobs or anything else. They will choose to either do something else or continue with the disliked job if they are benefiting from it in a way that makes it worth it to them. They will see all fields, subjects, occupations, neighborhoods, etc., as possibilities for them to pursue. They are extremely confident in their abilities. Even when I doubt them and worry about their futures, they calm my fears with their self-confidence. They will carry their childlike wonder and curiosity and excitement about the world with them into adulthood. Do I seem optimistic? Only time will tell, but these are the reasons we are unschooling. I really believe these things about Caleb and Jordan. —*Susan,* Iowa

I look back at my own education and can only laugh. The characteristic I most prized in myself as a student was efficiency; I was a master at doing the absolute bare minimum of work necessary to keep my straight-A average. I knew the rules and was very good at the whole game, and even though I knew it was a game, and frequently felt like a fraud, I also bought into the whole idea that I was a better person than those with the lower grades who didn't play this particular game as well. It took me a good ten years out of college to learn how to ask questions for myself, how to really learn. And that's something my kids already grasp completely; think what a gift of time that is for them! —*Ann,* California

Whether it has affected us or our kids more is hard to tell. I wonder what Allyson would be like if she had to deal with school. The mental image I get is not a positive one. I think about what I would do with my time if she were in school, and frankly, I would probably be volunteering for everything under the sun at the school just to keep my eye on things!

I think that, as adults, my kids will be able to think for themselves. They question everything. They are able to follow their internal rhythms for things (hunger, going to the bathroom) rather than the "herd-ing" that goes on in school, so I think they'll be more tuned in to their bod-ies. They won't get bogged down quite as much in peer pressure. I think this is especially important with raising a girl, since so much of their self-esteem can come from peer pressure and the media. —*Terri*, Colorado

Social Implications

Those of us who are involved with state or local homeschool support groups, or who subscribe to the Home Ed or Unschooling lists, quickly get used to what I think of as "pedagogical junk mail." At fre-quent intervals—usually at least quarterly—we receive letters that read something like this:

I am a credentialed elementary school teacher with more than ten years' experience working with students in (pick one) reading/writing/ arithmetic/foreign language/etc. Over my years in the classroom I've developed an amazing and innovative (pick one) phonics/penmanship/ math-facts/irregular-verb drill program that's guaranteed to teach any child effectively. I'm hoping your organization will help me publicize this product that I'm sure all your member families would find essential to their children's education.

Or sometimes the writer is more interested in providing profes-sional services than selling a product:

I've recently chosen to leave the public school classroom after a decade's experience, in favor of offering my expertise to homeschooling families like those of your organization. I'm sure there are many parents in your organization who are looking for professionals to provide their children with *quality* educational experiences, and I'd appreciate your putting me in touch with them.

Somehow they get it into their heads that we poor benighted unschooling parents can't possibly have the skills or even the interest to help our kids learn, and that we are waiting impatiently for their professional services to be visited upon us—for a fee, of course. What would those teachers say if they knew that most of us firmly believe that unschooling has a lot to offer conventional schools?

Just ask the second-most-asked question (after "What about socialization?") that unschoolers hear: "What if everybody did it?" Watch the smiles spread on our faces and brace yourself for the answers that pour out. A formal version of this inquiry is the second part of the questionnaire question I mentioned earlier: "Do you see unschooling ideas as having anything to offer society at large? What changes could unschooling ideas provoke?"

I see unschooling as something that forces the reweaving of family and extended family and community—precisely what seems to be most threatened by the way our society has been working for some decades. We don't arbitrarily categorize people into narrow age-classes, and the kids are comfortable with friends who are years older—and the older ones seem to be comfortable with younger friends, too.

I see this as teaching the very values that we talk about needing: creativity, independence, problem-solving, individual solutions.

School, as we're familiar with it, is a rather new idea in human history—and in its current form, only several decades old. It doesn't appear to have done very well at academic education, and it's done very poorly at the social aspects. Mass production hasn't turned out good people; the common view seems to be that good, successful people are so despite their school experience.

Unschooling is a way to achieve goals by people-sized, people-oriented means. —*Patrick*, California

I think that as unschooling becomes more widely known and our children begin to make their mark on the world, there is the potential for benefit to society as a whole. I think we can teach the world another way of understanding childhood—and adulthood, for that matter. I think we can show the success of not rushing our children into adult decisions before they are ready, of allowing them to develop each at their own pace and in their own way. And the effect of that is people who are more fully human, more likely to reach their potential, more at peace with themselves—people with positive energy to transform things and to find the desperately needed creative solutions to today's challenges. I would hope for a reversal of the dehumanizing aspects of society. —*Carol,* Florida

I get really depressed reading about proposals for educational reforms and watching which bandwagon all the politicians jump on each legislative session. They talk about how the schools aren't working, how kids are alienated from society, how kids don't have the good habits they need to be competent, useful workers. And all the reforms they propose—tougher curriculum standards, more standardized testing, longer school days and calendars, daytime curfews, and more—just exacerbate the problems they're meant to solve. Why not try something completely different? Unschooling—giving kids the opportunity to find what they care about, what they're good at—might be just the difference that's needed. —*Ann,* California

Unschooling touches on many societal issues. The farther we get into it, the more I start to look at other social institutions. I find myself wondering how much longer we will let ourselves be forced into jumping through hoops of all sorts. Why, for example, should an eighteen- or twenty-year-old have to present records, "grades," and accomplishments from three years back to show that she's an acceptable candidate for learning to be a veterinarian or a lawyer? Why does she then have to take classes that will never in any way enter into her chosen profession once she's working at it? Unschooling is creating independent thinkers and learners who can see through some of the unchallenged issues that restrict us as a society. What's more, as we're empowered in our own uniqueness, we are more aware of everyone else's uniqueness—a realization that provides more capacity for tolerance and flexibility in many areas of life. —*Lillian,* California

I would love to see public school become more unschoolish. I think there's too much emphasis placed on learning math and reading early. *Given a supportive environment,* kids pick these up naturally. It pains me to hear parents lamenting that their six-year-old can't read or is having problems in math. I've heard of unschooling kids who didn't bother learning to read until they were twelve, and then took off with it. Had they been in public school, the ridicule and pressure would have ensured they never loved reading.

I cringe when I hear someone say "Kids just don't understand how important school is." Kids do know what's important to them. Given the freedom to explore the world—and a supportive, nurturing environment—they will learn a tremendous amount. Yet they're locked into school, reading about Herbert Hoover since it's 1:15 P.M. and time for history class, and all sixth-graders are "supposed" to be taught American history, whether they're interested then or not.

I have no idea how this would work in a public-school setting (though Sudbury Valley School manages it). But I think it's essential to most kids' educational health. —*Joyce,* Massachusetts

If our society truly wants children to learn and become a functioning part of our culture, there is a lot to learn from the ideas of unschooling. At the top of the list would be *that children want to become capable adults.* It is an instinct. Second, timetables and age-appropriate curricula are only guidelines. Children learn in starts and stops, following their own timetables, and that is okay. I love the quote "Life is not a race but an adventure." Stop worrying and labeling children because they don't follow someone's timeline. Also, too many people are scared of kids because they have never seen what they're about. School can severely separate children and adults so that neither knows what the other is about. How we view teenagers is frightening to me. Daytime curfews, no places to just be with friends, no chance to take their time to discover who they are, few adults as mentors. Society really feels a need to try to control teenagers, and I think it will do serious harm to all of us. —*Emilie,* Washington

Unschooling ideas have much to offer society, but they are very threatening in their audacity, simplicity, and direction. People are afraid of personal freedoms, of unstructured time, of a lack of institutions to guide them through life, of what might happen if things aren't controlled for them. One of the things I respect about our country is its ability to embrace so much diversity. I don't see this happening in other countries so much; I see it becoming endangered in our country. Although many things are structured and monitored, institutionalized, packaged, we still have the opportunity as individuals to live mostly the way we want to live. I don't want to see this precious freedom become restricted, become extinct. Of course, unschooling is the antithesis of this trend, so I would like to see it flourish. —*Liane*, California

> Unschooling ideas have much to offer society, but they are very threatening in their audacity, simplicity, and direction. People are afraid of personal freedoms, of unstructured time, of a lack of institutions to guide them through life, of what might happen if things aren't controlled for them.

The idea of a world of people who have been unschooled is mind-boggling. Is "heaven" too strong a term to use for what such a world would be like? "Utopia"? Everyone pursuing interests separately and together without coercion, bribes, or threats? Fewer people being made to feel bored or stupid? It sounds great to me. —*Susan*, Iowa

It all boils down to a truth quickly learned by most families who decide to try "just partly unschooling." They may manage for a while to keep the unschooling approach limited to only a few subject areas, but unschooling ideas are insidious; they sneak and slither their way into every part of your life. The learning theory that you meant to apply just to the kids is indeed highly contagious. You begin to realize that you're envying your children the enthusiasm and eagerness with which they explore their world, and you realize that unschooling ideas are just as applicable to your own life. And then, of course, you're hooked for good. Once you've unschooled your children and yourselves, you begin to wonder how to apply unschooling ideas to other areas of your lives, to your work and your community.

We look at our communities and wonder why the ideas that seem so obvious to us are so strange to the rest of the population. Why does our society increasingly try to keep our children separate from the rest of society, from what will become the locus of their everyday lives once they reach adulthood? In our zeal to rescue children from exploitation, from child labor and unsafe living conditions, why have we moved so far to the other extreme—to keeping the workings of adult life completely out of the view of most children, even of older adolescents?

That so many children become lost when they reach the legal age of majority shouldn't be surprising. With all their years in school, with classes and assignments scheduled throughout for them, when and where do most children get a chance to feel useful, to create a meaningful place for themselves? They're considered too young, too immature, too unreliable, too untrustworthy to be allowed to do much of any real value; it's no wonder so many turn to their peers for affirmation and respect. We "protect" them from doing anything much in the way of real, meaningful work, deny them the opportunity to find places where they are truly needed, and then turn around and blame them for never doing anything worthwhile. If school is to prepare our kids for that archetypal real world, why are other schools the only places in that real world that are even remotely like school? Why don't we make more room for our children in every aspect of our society, welcome them into our everyday lives and work?

In many ways, unschooling can be reduced to that hoary old chestnut from the sixties—the one you still see occasionally on bumper stickers today: "Question Authority!" Ask why we always do things the way we've always done them, but ask with an open mind. Figure out what works and what doesn't, and use what works.

Most of us who occasionally ponder that second-most-asked question—what if everybody unschooled?—don't have any real answers. What would such a society be like? What if we did not classify

Some thoughts on unschooling I wrote up when I was fourteen:

Unschooling . . . for me it conjures up prisms, paradoxes, and unlimited travel. Time well spent and freedom. The "un" in life.

Have you ever stood at a window and looked at something happening on the other side? Have you ever thought that it looked inviting and fun? And yet at the same time, you know you cannot enter. You cannot get to the other side.

That is school. A place where you are shut up and can only see the world through a dark, twisted, distorted, and foggy window. And your world, your life, is being caged within four walls where it is desperately cold. And you wish you could get outside.

When you were little, perhaps you dreamed of being with fairies or witches, or with leprechauns and finding gold at the end of the rainbow. And you believed that it was possible to dance and sing with them—you just weren't ever at the right place or time. Or perhaps you were, perhaps you were lucky and you did get to dance and sing, and you did get a taste of that life.

But now you are still desperately trying to look out that twisted window to watch the comings and goings of the world outside. Maybe someday you decide to follow a new passage, and maybe you haven't lost all your curiosity about the world. You steer off the chosen path, a different hallway, a light at the end of the tunnel, a way out. But the journey there is not easy. The land beyond may be fruitful and ripe for the picking, but getting there is not easy. You discover that, unlike when you were in that confined world, here you must journey, and it is the journey that matters, not so much the end result. Before, you just went from one place to another without really thinking about where you were going or why. It was easier not to think and just to follow.

But you have chosen this new path, and though it is hard at first, it does get better, and you know somewhere within you that tomorrow *will* be better than today. You have started on a path that will take you to endless possibilities, and who knows where you will end up? As you travel, you meet countless people—some like yourself who are free and some who are still standing behind that invisible glass. For that is all the warped and twisted window was; it never really existed.

You were just told that it was there. You believed that it was there and never questioned otherwise. And to you, the people standing in the invisible boxes, behind those invisible, non-existent windows seem terribly silly. And yet you remember how easy it is to believe, how it was not so long ago that you were just like them, and you feel sorry that they haven't found the light.

But you have chosen a better path, a path for the picking. Though it will not always be the easiest, smoothest path, it is the path you chose; no one else chose it for you. Ahead of you lie countless hills, bends and turns in the road, paradoxes and possibilities. You are one of those they call unschoolers, and you are *free!* —*Chase, Florida*

---

and categorize children according to their age and the facility with which they acquire skills? What if we worked from their strengths instead of concentrating on their weaknesses? What if every person discovered and pursued at least one passion, one positive interest that consumed them to the point where they became expert at it (or at least found joy in the search)? What would being a part of such a community be like?

It's certainly an intriguing idea. I intend to find out.

Resources

Arons, Stephen. *Short Route to Chaos: Conscience, Community, and the Re-Constitution of American Schooling* (University of Massachusetts Press, 1997). Arons criticizes current educational reform proposals, such as Goals 2000. He believes that education should be a matter of conscience within families, without government oversight or regulation of content.

Berliner, David C., and Bruce J. Biddle. *The Manufactured Crisis: Myths, Frauds, and the Attack on America's Public Schools* (Addison-Wesley, 1995). Don't let the title of this book mislead you into believing that the authors think there are no problems in American schools today; they simply believe that most of the critics are proposing solutions for the wrong problems.

Coontz, Stephanie. *The Way We Never Were: American Families and the Nostalgia Trap* (Basic Books, 1993). Coontz is a family historian who compares our beliefs with the reality of family life in the past, and considers some of the problems caused by basing social policy on such misconceptions.

Dominguez, Joe, and Vicki Robin. *Your Money or Your Life: Transforming Your Relationship with Money and Achieving Financial Independence* (Penguin Books, 1993). Not simply a guide to financial management, this book advises taking a good look at what you want out of life and whether your job and financial habits actually hinder achieving those goals.

Fogler, Michael. *Un-Jobbing: The Adult Liberation Handbook* (Free Choice Press, 1997). Fogler and his wife wanted a more sensible lifestyle centered around their family, so they quit their jobs and figured out how to make ends meet in a less stressful fashion.

Holt, John. *Instead of Education: Ways to Help People Do Things Better* (Holt Associates, 1988). For Holt, learning is doing, and it is something we ought to be able to make easier for everyone, whether child or adult.

Holt, John. *Escape from Childhood: The Rights and Needs of Children* (Holt Associates, 1996). Holt's classic on children's rights will get you wondering just what is so wonderful about childhood, when you consider how our society treats kids.

Levine, David, Robert Lowe, Bob Peterson, and Rita Tenorio, eds. *Rethinking Schools: An Agenda for Change* (The New Press, 1995). This anthology of articles from the education reform journal *Rethinking Schools* offers a good overview of current issues in progressive education reform.

Males, Mike A. *The Scapegoat Generation: America's War on Adolescents* (Common Courage Press, 1996). Males takes a startling, infuriated look at how politicians, the media, and others routinely misinterpret statistics about American youth, and at the results of blaming many of our most pressing social problems on the actual victims of those problems.

CONTRIBUTORS

The families who completed the questionnaire for this book represent fifty-seven children who have been unschooling for over two hundred kid-years.

Amy, Idaho, lives with her husband and their daughters (six, five, and three). She worked as a copyeditor and magazine production manager until her first child was born, and is now a full-time homemaker. Her husband is finishing an accounting degree and works as an office manager. The children have always unschooled.

Andrea, Nevada, is a full-time mom, and her husband is an Air Force master sergeant. They have a ten-year-old son and an eight-year-old daughter; both have been unschooling since leaving public school last year.

Ann, California, is a part-time writer, and her husband is a software engineer. They live in northern California with their two always-unschooled daughters (nine and thirteen).

Carol B., Florida, and her husband (an immunology professor) have unschooled their kids since 1988, when their son was almost six and their daughter was almost nine.

Carol E., California, is a retired registered nurse who's recently closed her family-based daycare business; her husband is chief financial officer for an international service business. Their younger daughter just entered a private school for sixth grade, while their older daughter continues unschooling.

Carolyn, Pennsylvania, and her husband are both in the computer business—she with a small desktop publishing business, and he as a computer security specialist. Their eleven-year-old daughter and eight-year-old son have unschooled for two years.

Cathy B., California, lives with her husband in a mountain town in Northern California and unschools her nine-year-old son.

Cathy R., Pennsylvania, is starting a home-based sales business. Her husband is a college professor and part-time farmer. Their children—two boys (ten and four) and one girl (eight)—have always unschooled.

Chase, Florida, is Carol B.'s eighteen-year-old daughter. She has been accepted for admission by all three colleges she applied to and is now considering her options for life beyond unschooling.

Cindy, Wisconsin, and her husband both have engineering backgrounds. Currently, he works full-time and she is employed part-time. Their two sons (twelve and nine) have always unschooled.

Emilie, Washington, and her husband live in a small town with their two sons (nine and four), who have always unschooled.

Grace, California, and her husband are both in the computer business—she from home and he outside the home. Their two children (eight and five) have always unschooled.

Jill, California, is a single mother of three teenagers, all unschooled all their lives, all beginning to strike out on their own.

Jo, Louisiana, is a self-employed computer consultant. Her husband is a financial consultant with a brokerage firm. Their eight-year-old son and seven-year-old daughter have always unschooled.

Joanne, Virginia, and her husband are biologists. Jenny, their sixteen-year-old daughter, has always homeschooled.

Joyce, Massachusetts, trained as an electrical engineer but now works as a full-time mom and part-time writer. Her husband works full-time as a manufacturing manager. Their six-year-old daughter has unschooled since she left preschool.

Kathy, Illinois, a former biology teacher, currently works part-time as a tutor; her husband is a software engineer. They recently moved from a Chicago suburb to a small rural town. Their sons (eight and five) have always unschooled.

Laura D., Texas, and her husband, John, have two children (six and four). Although they are based in Texas, they travel extensively because of John's work as a motion-picture production sound mixer.

Laura Y., California, and her husband live in southern California. She is a full-time mom; he works as a driver-courier for an armored car company. Their eight-year-old son and six-year-old daughter have unschooled for a year, after leaving public school to homeschool the previous year.

Liane, California, is a full-time mom married to a chiropractor. Their two twelve-year-old daughters began homeschooling in third grade, but began unschooling after fourth grade.

Lillian, California, lives in a small northern California town with her husband, an airline pilot, and their fifteen-year-old son, who has unschooled since second grade.

Linda, New York, is an at-home mom; her husband works at home as a computer programmer for an out-of-state company. They decided on unschooling before their children—two boys (ten and seven) and one girl (four)—were born.

Marianne, Arizona, and her husband (a fire battalion chief) have two daughters (eleven and eight). They have homeschooled since preschool, but only began unschooling about a year ago.

Melissa, California, and her husband live in a small northern California city with their four children (fourteen, twelve, ten, and eight). He works as an engineer; she is active in local politics and with a statewide homeschool organization. The kids have unschooled all their lives, although the oldest recently opted to try high school for ninth grade.

Patrick, California, is a former technical writer, now an at-home dad. His wife is a biochemist. They planned to unschool their two sons (five and three) before the elder one was born.

Ruth, Montana, and her husband, a mining engineer, live in a small town with their twelve-year-old son and ten-year-old daughter. They began unschooling two years ago, after attending a private alternative school.

Samantha, Texas, and her husband, a software developer, consider that their two-year-old daughter has been unschooling all her life.

Sandra, New Mexico, is a former teacher married to a computer-graphics engineer. Their three children (eleven, ten, and six) have always unschooled.

Sean, California, is Melissa's oldest child, who opted at fourteen to attend a Catholic high school after previously unschooling.

Stefani, New Hampshire, with a master's degree in oboe performance, plays in an orchestra and teaches music, while her husband is a software contractor. They live in a small town with their ten-year-old daughter. They began homeschooling with a structured approach when she was halfway through second grade, and "slid into unschooling the end of last year."

Susan, Iowa, lives in a small town with her husband, son (fourteen), and daughter (eleven). She works full-time coordinating a local college reading program while her husband is at home with the kids, who have always unschooled.

Terri, Colorado, lives on fifteen acres in a passive-solar house with her husband, seven-year-old daughter, and two-year-old son. Terri has a degree in business; her husband is an engineer. The children have always unschooled.

Terry, British Columbia, is a children's book author; her husband is a musician. Their oldest daughter (now twenty-six and on her own) began unschooling after a week and a half of kindergarten and continued until college; their second daughter (twenty) began school with sixth grade, skipped seventh, graduated with honors from a fine arts high school, and recently finished her first year of college; their third daughter (eleven) has always unschooled.

INDEX